ADAM BUDE is an extraordinarily successful sales pro and entrepreneur with nearly three decades of direct sales, marketing and business experience. He has led, coached, mentored and inspired thousands of salespeople and business owners globally, while continually generating over seven-figure annual returns for the companies he has operated and partnered with. He prides himself on his honesty, integrity and authenticity when it comes to sales and leadership and through the messages in this book, he wants to change the way sales are carried out in the world.

THE ART OF
Authentic
SELLING

THE ART OF *Authentic* SELLING

Stop selling ... Be of service ...
Lead Authentically

ADAM BUDE

Published by Bluestar Publishing
www.theartofauthenticselling.com

First published 2021
© 2021 Adam Bude

The moral right of the author has been asserted.

All rights reserved.

Without limiting the rights under copyright restricted above, no part of this publication may be reproduced, stored in or introduced into a retrieval system, or transmitted, in any form or by any means (electronic, mechanical, photocopying, recording or otherwise), without the prior written permission of the copyright owner and publisher of this book.

 A catalogue record for this book is available from the National Library of Australia

ISBN 978 0 6450484 0 7 (pbk)
ISBN 978 0 6450484 1 4 (ebk)

Edited by Gail Tagarro, editors4you
Designed and typeset by Helen Christie, Blue Wren Books
Photos by Paul Henry Photography
Printed by Ingram Spark

What makes you matter? Being true to yourself and your vision takes strength. Taking one step towards your vision each day takes commitment. Pushing through adversity takes courage, but the rewards of following through authentically are magical. Make all your decisions based on what makes your heart sing to create a brighter NOW. Forget your past stories, and current circumstances.

ADAM BUDE

CONTENTS

	Acknowledgments	xi
	Introduction	1
1	Sales … Let's Get Started	15
2	The Winning Mindset	21
3	Just Be YOU	41
4	What Do You Believe?	55
5	Create Your Results by Design	65
6	How Can I Be of Service?	75
7	Get Into Bed with the Right Company	83
8	Creating Connection	95
9	STOP Chewing My Ears Off	105
10	I am Not Afraid of You	115
11	The Plan of Attack	123
12	The Game!	131
	My Recommended Reading List	155

ACKNOWLEDGMENTS

There have been so many people who have influenced my life, in both positive and negative ways. All of them have helped shape my future direction and forged who I am in my ever-evolving journey of life and business.

I will have to start with my wife Amanda. She has been there right from the beginning of my sales and business career. She has been my rock, my sounding board, my number one critic and greatest fan. They say behind every great man, is a better woman. That is for sure in my case! (Had to say that, I'm sure she'll read this …) Seriously, I would not be who I am today, or be doing what I do today, if it wasn't for her. I owe so much to Amanda and love her to bits. I'm so incredibly grateful to have her on my side as we travel this journey of life together.

Of course, my parents. They did the best they could with the resources they had when raising me. My foundations came from them, my core identity was established through them and each of them has supported me in different ways. They have shown me what it's like to be a parent, and to have courage and commitment in life. My entrepreneurial spirit and drive come from my dad's family, and my vulnerability and emotion come from my mum's. The perfect balance.

My school teachers who unanimously said in most of my report cards, 'If only Adam applied himself ...' Well, they taught me to invest more time, energy and effort in what I was interested in, and to do what I needed to do, instead of just following the herd and becoming indoctrinated. I'm not a fan of the education system, but a huge fan of life experience. That is the best education you will ever get!

To all my managers, superiors, mentors and coaches in the business world who saw enough in me to give me a go. They helped educate, guide, support and groom me along the way, and I remain connected to many of them to this day. I have so much gratitude for these folks.

I consider a mentor, even if indirectly, every author and facilitator whose courses, seminars, books and podcasts I've read, listened to or attended. If not for your vision, I could not have become who I am today. So thank you!

Unlearning everything I knew about sales and learning to sell with authentic leadership in my first business venture was an amazing transition.

To every person I have had the privilege to coach, train and mentor (both directly and indirectly) and who has expressed their appreciation and gratitude to me — you guys inspire me daily to keep showing up. To be more than I am and to push through all my life challenges to be better, so I can pave the way for others to follow.

My friends in life, who have come and gone, all have had an impact on me. Thank you!

ACKNOWLEDGMENTS

To all the bullies, knockers, naysayers and keyboard warriors, in and out of business, you too have had a very positive influence on me and for that, I am forever grateful.

My first dogs Saki and Sumo who taught me the value of loyalty and unconditional love. To keep showing up every day with a smile and excitement for what it might bring. Just the best. Love you guys to bits. Our new dog Jedi will continue that for years to come.

And lastly my three amazing kids, Amelia, Josh and Bree. I get out of bed every day for you guys. We have the opportunity to live a great life together filled with endless experiences, laughter and fun, creating lifelong memories for us all. You guys are my legacy and with Amanda, my life!

INTRODUCTION

Thank you for choosing to buy and read my book *The Art of Authentic Selling*. Much gratitude!

The Art of Authentic Selling is the culmination of my life's work. I began my sales career back in the 1990s, working in retail at the ripe old age of 20-something.

Nothing too glamorous back then, I can assure you. Stocking shelves, working long boring hours for the worst pay ever while having to be polite to customers … However, after some meaningless jobs, I found myself at an auto parts company and was soon forging a semi-solid career in the automotive industry. Because of my reputation at the time, I was poached from them by a competitor that expanded into Victoria. That was my first introduction into what I thought was proper sales, becoming a sales rep. I always had good rapport with customers and funnily enough, always exceeded my targets.

One day, while I was out seeing a client, I got 'the' phone call to come in for an urgent meeting. When I got there, I was told to clear out the car and hand back my keys, and given a cheque for one month's wages. I had been retrenched and I couldn't believe it! Our entire company shut down just like that and we were all escorted off the premises. After that, I was unemployed for six months. The reality of not having any formal qualifications after I left high school hit. I was virtually unemployable.

Back at school, I had been bored. I was one of those kids lost in the system, uninspired to think too much about what I wanted to do in the future, except make money. I was in trouble regularly and found myself sitting at the front of the class. I hated being forced to learn French and history and half the rubbish that came with maths and science, thinking to myself back then, *When am I ever going to need this shit!* I was more interested in playing football and cricket and goofing around.

I remember every parent-teacher interview going something like this: 'If only Adam applied himself ...' In fact, my year 10 coordinator, Mr L., told me to leave school and get a job, because I was never going to pass or amount to anything anyways! Well at that point, I decided to stick it to him, continue and pass my high school. Which I did.

Being unemployed was a crappy time in my life. I started feeling a little depressed, but ironically it was my first real turning point. My sales career started after the company closed down.

One night at my cousin's flat in Elwood, we were talking about finding another job while drinking a beer and smoking a joint, as you do in your 20s. Jez said, 'Ads, you've always been good at sales, why don't you get a commission-only job? That way you can make as much money as you want!'

INTRODUCTION

That was one of those light-bulb moments, something that I remember so clearly, and the next day I started looking for commission-only opportunities.

The idea of working for commission only didn't seem so foreign at the time because I had an entrepreneurial mindset anyway. My parents and grandparents had always been business owners. So, it felt like a natural path to take. As is stood, what else could I do?

I looked through the classifieds in the paper and saw an advert with a picture of two eyes staring at me. It said something along the lines of, 'Imagine yourself making a six-figure income'. It was a commission-only role promising earning potential of $100k plus. The most I had ever earned up to that point was $35k and a company car. It was a direct sales role in the investment seminar industry. Around that time, I read my first personal development book, *Rich Dad, Poor Dad* by Robert Kiyosaki. *Far out, could this be a sign from the universe?* I asked myself.

I was 28 years old and had no right looking for work of that calibre, but I thought, *What have I got to lose?* and applied.

A few days later my phone rang and I was granted an interview. It was the first in months, so I went. I sat down in a boardroom full of candidates. As it turned out we were all being interviewed together, a 'last man standing' kind of thing. And I got through. A few days later I had a second interview with the director and was offered a position.

I hadn't earned anything for ages and was receiving unemployment benefits at the time, so it seemed like the government was paying me to learn something new. After some initial training, I thought, *I am so far over my head here.* This was big, there was too much to learn, so much pressure, sales consultants leaving every day and the recruitment cycle happening every week. Where I'd thought I was special, I realised that this industry was a man-eater! Sink or swim.

One month passed, no sales. Second month passed, no sales. Third month passed and still no sales. Even though it was commission only, I was on a drawback retainer system, meaning they were paying me an upfront wage, which would all be deducted from my future commissions. After three months of no sales, I was close to owing them nearly 9k! Freaking out, broke and now in debt for the first time, I was given another two weeks to prove myself. Otherwise I was out, and they wanted all their money back.

Then, I got a sale. Then another one and then another. It was like the rabbit and the tortoise, with me being the tortoise. I was starting to get the hang of this hard-selling thing. And my ego loved it. I was cocky and rude at one point with a 'do anything you can' approach to get the deal done. No sale = No pay.

The company was ruthless, wanting more and more. We started work at 7.30 am and were still doing evening appointments until 11 pm at times. The programs we sold were property investment seminars ranging from 15k to 55k and it was hard selling. We did everything we could to ensure every possible person who walked through our doors signed up. At the end, my closing rate was one in every three.

The company at one point even ran an internal promotion for six months that would have seen me receive a 50k cash bonus for selling $2 million worth of courses.

INTRODUCTION

We needed to close 130 sales in that time frame to qualify, and everybody had to do this! (I was so dumb. On what planet does EVERYONE hit their target?)

We started off with over twenty consultants and at the end only eight of us remained. Only four people achieved the target and I was one of them. A 5k consolation prize came my way, so I took my then girlfriend, now wife Amanda, on a holiday and bought myself my first TAG Heuer watch. A limited edition Sea Racer.

That was my first six-figure annual income, and I finished the year earning 120k in commission. Not too shabby for someone who was not qualified or experienced at anything, and whose last job had paid him 35k! It really was a quantum leap for me.

That job ended up fizzling out as the company closed. I saw first-hand what happens when you do unethical things to people in business. Eventually, it all comes back and bites you on the arse!

So the hunt began again and I was offered a job at a stock market advisory service selling stock recommendation and trading packages. That lasted about six months because it too was unethical, and the company owners had a big falling out! They were making so much money, it was ridiculous. What made things worse, while I was there, I learned a little bit about trading CFDs and was again too cocky because under good instruction, I put all of my money, and more, on an overnight trade that couldn't lose! I had one long position on the NAB and a short position on BHP.

The mining and banking industries at the time were counteracting each other. Pending an expected bad announcement of gold that night in the States, share prices would go up or down. And then, unexpectedly, the Japanese railway was bombed that night and the stock market went into turmoil. My positions were closed out and not only did I lose all my money, but I owed the brokers money on top! I was broke, in debt and now homeless because we didn't have the money to pay rent.

What made things worse was that because of it, we had to cancel our wedding, borrow money to pay back the brokers, move to a cheaper place to live in and live off credit cards. The wind was knocked out of my sails. It was screwed!

So, what do I do next? I asked myself. *Look for another way to make 'quick' money?* I found myself answering a telesales ad for a 'publishing company', selling magazines for not-for-profit entities. Sounded reputable. I got offered a job on the spot (first alarm bell) and had to rebuild. But I hated it. Selling advertising space in the form of sponsorships to get the magazines out to the members free of charge was the spin. Truth was, it was just a money-making spin for the company owners, and the salespeople made 22–30% commission on each sale. But I had no choice. No qualifications or trade to fall back on, I felt locked in. Luckily, I had a completely different mindset from the others who worked there, as that industry generally attracts rough diamonds and the unemployable.

In saying that, I am grateful, as my management career started there. I was one of their best trainers and built a solid team. It opened my eyes to the call centre environment. It was, however, soul-destroying. I was verbally abused almost every day by the people I called and by my staff!

INTRODUCTION

Dealing with rough diamonds and pretty much begging for money from small business owners was just the pits.

And again, no sale, no money. It was a big fight every week, but I did what I had to do and was still one of their best ever salespeople. In my best year there, I earned 140k. A CEO's wage in some industries. Unfortunately, I got a glimpse of the other side of direct sales and it was not for me! I was trading my values and integrity for money. So as soon as we were back on our feet, I quit.

I took a few weeks off to recharge and thought getting a job would be easy because I'd done some of the hardest versions of sales. Wrong. The corporate world didn't recognise this type of work and I was again unemployed for over six months! It was the worst time of my life. Our first-born Amelia was around one year old, I had no job and we started living off unemployment benefits not long after.

It gets better. Amanda fell pregnant again. At the ultrasound appointment, our obstetrician congratulated us. My heart dropped because all I could think about was, *Shit, how am I going to pay for this?* Then he said, 'Wait, do you see what I see?' I said, 'What do you see?' He said, 'THERE'S TWO!'

F#*K ME.

Instead of being excited, I felt sick. He asked me, 'What do you do for a living?' I replied, 'Nothing, I quit my job last week.' Good times.

I was starting to feel the reality of what long-term job-seekers go through, and it's horrible. Finally, I got a break. I nailed a job with a company from Sydney in the corporate hospitality sector. They sold hospitality packages to tier 1 and tier 2 fortune-500 companies at the CEO, CFO and MD levels for major sporting bodies at live events. We represented The Australian Open Tennis, Cricket Victoria, NSW Cricket, NRL (National Rugby League) FFA (Football Federation of Australia) and the ARU (Australian Rugby Union). They loved the fact that I liked to fend for myself; it was exactly the person they were looking for to head up their expanding Melbourne operations. It was still in direct sales, but for the first time I got to experience senior level corporate B2B (business to business) sales. All my other work had been B2C (business to consumer). I started on a $100k base, plus comms! Up until then, my $100k-plus earnings had all come from commission only. I was to start recruiting a sales force in our Melbourne office and I was excited for the first time in a long time.

It was mid 2008 when I started and not long after, Josh and Bree were born. That was when the fun really started. Guess what world event happened that year? The Global Financial Crisis! Shit — here we go again! The first thing companies stopped spending their money on was discretionary spending like client relationships and corporate functions. It was a complete no-go zone. We battled through month after month. I had hired and trained several salespeople, who obviously couldn't cut it. It was new business development and all phone based. But the times were the times. I was assured my position was safe, but really, for how long? I already knew the feeling of no job security and was frightened of going through that experience again.

Month after month, my salary was reducing so that the company could keep me on. I was still getting sales, but not enough. I was sitting in a serviced office in Melbourne's CBD all by myself. I needed to hit my targets in order to keep us afloat financially at the worst possible time, with newborn twins and in the most unfavourable economic climate to sell in.

Adding to my financial pressure was the fact that Josh and Bree were extremely sick babies, with many food allergies and sleeping issues, so we were always at the doctor's. More bills for me and less sleep for me sent me spiralling out of control. I fell into post-natal depression. I couldn't cope. It felt as if the whole universe was against me. I hated my responsibilities and I hated the life I was dealt and I was ready to end it all. I stood every morning at the train station looking at the trains coming by and ready to jump.

I reached a new low and medical intervention took over.

I remember looking into the eyes of my eldest daughter Amelia one night while the meds were kicking in and all I saw was love and light. For the first time in months I saw past all the dark. That was the spark I needed to pick myself up off the ground and start again — again!

The Ashes were on and I was working at the boxing day test match at the MCG. My boss was down from Sydney and we got talking. I told him about my depression and that I was considering relocating to Queensland to start over. After some open conversations, he mentioned they would look at relocating me. It all seemed good.

After the test match finished, we headed to Port Douglas in tropical north Queensland for my brother's wedding. The whole family was going, and because I was going through a tough time and not coping with life very well, we thought it would do us good to have a small break. We were looking forward to the family helping by looking after the kids some of the time. This didn't happen; we were totally on our own. The lack of support helped make up my mind and I said to Amanda, 'That's it, we're out of here, and we're moving to Queensland.'

When I got back to work, my boss told me that head office in Europe had said no to the Brisbane office. They wanted the Melbourne office to stay and didn't want to expand. That left me no choice but to resign, as I had already decided to move.

I looked for jobs and teed up two interviews, one in Brisbane as a corporate sales manager with the Brisbane Lions Football Club and another in phone sales with a stock market advisory company on the Gold Coast. Unfortunately, I was too late for the first role which I was most interested in, as they had already selected someone, however, I got offered the phone sales job on the spot with the stock market company (another alarm bell). I knew it was a massive step back for me, but also that it was important to have a job before we moved. So I took it. Four weeks later, we were living on the Gold Coast.

I hit the ground running at the stock market job. I knew how to sell and within three months of being there, my on-target earnings were looking like being $200k. I ended up earning the most I had earned in my career to date, finishing the year off at $160k. But it was a lot of pressure closing over the phone and I learned very quickly that we were ripping people off. The sales manager was the one making all the trade recommendations — we didn't even have a qualified stock market analyst! The target market was retirees or those close to retiring looking for more money. How they captured the leads was disgusting. Blatantly misleading people.

Customers would come through as a lead, we would do a one-hour phone presentation and they would pay $5k for our service on the spot or by Friday, because that was when our 'special promo' finished! Plus, they had to invest a minimum of $10k into a trading account. Most of those people lost every cent. To cap it off, the company kept playing with the commission structures, making it almost impossible to hit our new targets. I was stuck in another dodgy direct sales job doing it all again for money.

When I learned about my people losing their money, I felt sick. My sales manager at the time said, 'Ads, these people all have money. They may as well give it to us before they give it to someone else. They will spend it anyways.'

What a fucked-up attitude was what I thought! To me, that was preying on the vulnerable and stealing from them. In fact, I said, 'How would you like it if you knew people were ripping your parents off?' That went down well …

The company changed its name four times while I was there because of internet slander and I felt that I had stooped to a new low with my sales career. It was hard selling, story-selling, fear-based selling and it was wrong. Again, my core values were rocked and my integrity was lost, all for the sake of getting a sale and making money.

So off I went again. This time I wanted to be self-employed and I WANTED OUT OF THE DIRECT SALES INDUSTRY FOR GOOD.

My wife Amanda introduced me to a friend of hers who had just started an online business, suggesting I take a look. It was a personal development company. Again, it was back in direct sales, but this time it was sales by leadership, not by 'closing the deal'. It was more of an anti-sell. People decided for themselves if they wanted to join, without any pushing. It had everything I thought I was looking for in a business model.

1. Online
2. High up-front profits
3. Leveraged income
4. Residual sales
5. A product that actually helped people
6. Home based
7. No limitations or restrictions
8. Not MLM
9. And — NO SELLING!

It was tough at first entering a new system with a different methodology of operation. When I first started, I was still using all the sales techniques from my Neuro Linguistic Programming (NLP) days and sales experience. Matching and mirroring, building rapport, guiding people and overcoming their objections, telling them why they would benefit from the product. Painting incredible pictures about how life could be so different … And after a few months of this, surprise, surprise, NO MONEY.

I listened to one of our training calls: 'When you get over the selling it phase, you'll make money.' That was when the light-bulb moment came. It was really hard 'unlearning' everything that had worked for me in sales. Selling through leadership, detachment, how we conduct ourselves when communicating with others, is at another level altogether — and in my opinion, the way sales as an industry needs to be moving forward. Hence the reason for this book. I want to change the way we look at sales globally!

It should no longer be just about the bottom line of companies. Do what you can do to get the deal and find ways to increase by add-ons, like, 'Would you like fries with that?' That is taking advantage of people. Asking them to buy something they don't want or need, instead of providing service and value.

> 'You can have everything you want in life, IF you will just help enough people get what they want.'
>
> ZIG ZIGLAR

After having the courage to back myself, quit the 9 to 5 job and play full out in my business, in March 2015 I had my first $50k US month! I made $50,000 US profit in a single month! More than I used to make in a year back in the automotive industry. The following May I had my first $100,000 US profit month! Since starting my business, I've sold several millions of dollars of products online!

When I started creating financial success in that business, I became part of a global leadership team. Not because of where my perceived leadership skills where at, but because

I was one of only a handful of people doing the work and getting some results.

Over the years I learned more and more about what leadership truly is in sales and in life, investing thousands of hours and dollars into my personal development. Subsequently, my growth and leadership really began to shine.

I have always been one to support, nourish and inspire people to be better. To lead from the front. Most important for me is my genuine belief in others, and showing them through my actions that what I achieve is also possible for them.

Sales leadership is not about financial success. It is not about who is bigger and better. It is not about 'fake it till you make it'. It is not about who is smarter or more attractive, and it's certainly not about how long you've been doing something. Mostly, it is not about winning at any cost or seeking recognition!

I went from being a retail assistant to an entrepreneur, speaker, mentor and now author. You are about to learn my idea of the difference between the old broken sales methods that are failing and the new sales methods through leadership. The difference is **'authentic selling'**.

My goal with this book is to help people connect back to their inner truth. To work and sell with the right intentions, integrity and authenticity and not be controlled by mediocre and outdated sales methods and tactics that are not appreciated by customers.

Chapter 1

SALES ...
LET'S GET STARTED

'Sales is not about selling anymore, but about building trust and education.'

SIVA DEVAKI

First, we need to define what sales is.

Sales is an exchange of a commodity or service for money. It is the lifeline of every business and the global economy. It is also the oldest known profession. And therein lies a fascinating question.

Why is it not spoken about in schools, or taught at university? Because it can't be. Sales requires skills, yes, but it is experience that makes all the difference.

Most decent sales jobs advertised on job sites (those that pay over $65k a year) require some sort of tertiary qualifications as a prerequisite — even though there are no formal qualifications available for this. Crazy! And most sales jobs I see pay less than admin jobs. What is that all about?

I've never heard anyone say that when they grow up, they want to be a great salesperson.

Why not?

Because there are so many different types of sales roles that the truth is, each industry and each organisation needs to train from within. Every business is managed differently so there can never be a one-stop shop. Look at pharmaceutical reps, or real estate agents, or retail sales, or IT and systems sales. Wholesale companies, car dealerships, government contract sales … the examples are endless.

Also, sadly, salespeople have never really been treated with respect. Most salespeople are treated as replaceable commodities. They have the fear of losing their jobs if they don't hit their KPIs. The pressure to perform is probably the greatest out of any role in the company, as the expectations from above are to sell, sell, sell their stuff to maximise bottom line turnover — whether the products are worthy or not.

Weekly sales meetings, monthly budgets, future forecasting are all based on increasing sales. And the worst part is, it is never, EVER, going to be enough. The more you achieve, the more that is expected from you, and ultimately, the less you will get paid for it! Every year the targets increase, the workload and expectations increase and in exchange the commissions decrease because companies are looking to improve the bottom line instead of rewarding the individuals for creating the business. Too often I hear of bonuses not being paid, commissions withheld and incentives altered. All this does is take away the inner drive from the salesperson to want to perform because deep down they all know, what is the point?

That happened to me so many times over my career. The more I sold, the more they wanted and more the commissions structures were adjusted. Worse was the BS spin that came with it each time they were changed, to justify why I should be paid less to perform more. Spare a thought for those who have no incentives other than keeping their jobs!

But here is the cold, hard truth. If your products and services are good, you do not need to employ people to cold call and canvas for business. We must continually prospect for new and repeat business in order to grow. Now, there is a much better way to do it through authenticity and integrity. In today's world, people want to do business with people they see, like and trust. The old sales world is changing for the better, and a new level of service and experience is required. It's about time too!

So how and why do people get into sales?

Most people fall into sales. They start off when they are young, at the bottom of the food chain. For example, you may have finished school or may still be in school. You could have gone on for higher level schooling, however, you were unable to land a role in your actual industry or field, and because people need a job, many will do anything. They may start in retail or customer service or hospitality, which are still a form of sales. They are menial jobs with minimum wages, simply because those jobs require little or no experience. Geez, imagine being excited about working for $12.50 an hour! But it is a start.

Others may have finished a degree in a specialised field and are working their way up from the bottom in their desired industry. They find themselves working super-hard and exceptionally long hours looking for promotions. By then they venture into other areas, such as specific or strategic sales in their field.

Like a close friend of mine, who went to university, got a degree in an area of IT, and is now working in a strategic sales role in IT for a global company. Massive pressure, long hours, high stress, big corporate deals and a multiple six-figure income. Flying here, travelling there. But is it worth it when he's missing out on life, constantly exhausted and verging on being burned out?

The problem then is, they are forced to stay in sales to keep up their lifestyle. It becomes a trap. They are committed, hooked — especially men. I don't know about you, but seriously, who can get excited about selling ink cartridges or coffee?

Most people do what they need to do to earn a living and meet their financial obligations. It then just becomes about the money. In most cases they sell their souls to their organisations because of the fear of losing their jobs, when in fact sales could be so much more ... Sales could be one of the most rewarding careers if done right. There is no greater feeling than genuinely helping people by providing a solution to their problems, in the right sales role, with the right company, while getting paid well for your time, efforts, skills and experience. Imagine doing this for a living! You would be feeding off your own energy daily, excited about meeting the next person.

So where can you find that fit?

Find an industry that excites you. Find a company whose values and ethics are in line with yours. Be a user of the products yourself so you become the greatest testimonial, and look for the opportunity where you can be rewarded.

I wrote this book because I believe the sales model needs to change for individuals, organisations and consumers. When salespeople are treated as a valued part of the business and they personally have skin in the game to achieve common goals, they become aligned, and that's where synergy hits.

I was also sick and tired of seeing bad salespeople take advantage of others just to make money. Their intentions are not right and that leads to companies and industries as a whole getting a very bad reputation, not to mention the individual.

From my experience, authentic selling is the only way to go. Understanding the needs of the client and knowing if you can add value and make a difference by supporting them. Providing service as the number one objective and aiming to deliver the result is a great platform for achieving a genuine business.

When everyone is in it together, for the same reasons, the magical outcomes flow and the word 'sales' means creating success.

Chapter 2

THE WINNING MINDSET

'Don't wish it were easier, wish you were better.'

JIM ROHN

MANAGING YOUR EMOTIONS

One of the toughest things about sales (and life for that matter) is managing your emotional state. When I first started my life in commission sales, the constant rejections affected my confidence and courage a lot. I took the rejections personally and emotionally, struggled daily to overcome them. You see, sales is all about prospecting, and if you are constantly being rejected and told no, sooner or later it can have an effect on you.

Strengthening your resilience is especially important. I highly recommend a great book titled *Go For No*, by Andrea

Waltz and Richard Fenton. However, the truth is that it takes an incredibly special person to be able to constantly handle rejection.

I have heard over the years the saying 'be like Teflon', meaning do not allow anything to stick, just let it bounce right off you. Easier said than done, which is why everyone hates cold calling or public speaking and why most people do not last in a sales role. It is just not in their personality.

I have a different point of view because sales is something everybody in every profession does, whether they are aware of it or not. The only difference is some people are labelled 'salesperson' because that is their specialised role. A sale is made in every human transaction. Either somebody sells you on their stuff, or you sell them on yours. Whenever someone is convinced or influenced to do something, they have been sold to.

For example, instead of looking for natural remedies, a doctor sells you on the fact you need a special medication; a friend convinces you to do something you wouldn't normally do; a police officer explains why you must abide by a certain law. As soon as we agree to something, we have been sold into it. From a purchasing point of view, more often than not, we really do not need or want it.

How do you feel when you go into a retail shop and the salesperson says, 'Can I help you with something?' or you are tele-marketed, or you know you are being upsold? Let us be honest, nobody likes it!

So, when the salesperson approaches, people naturally go into arms crossed and closed mind mode.

THE ROLE OF PERSONAL DEVELOPMENT

When I first realised this, I went on the path of personal development to help me improve not only my sales abilities, but also my own mindset. Over the years, my greatest investment has been on personal development courses, books, audios, podcasts, seminars and so on. I have invested hundreds of thousands of my personal money in order to become better at my craft and better in my mind.

In my early 20s I was fascinated about being wealthy and found myself reading *Think and Grow Rich* by Napoleon Hill: a must-read by the way. That led me to Robert Kiyosaki, the *Rich Dad* series, and when I started my first commission-only role, I evolved into stuff by Brian Tracey, Tom Hopkins, Brad Sugars, Zig Ziglar, Bob Proctor, Tony Robbins, Jim Rohn, Wayne Dyer, etc. I just could not get enough. Then I started reading autobiographies of extraordinarily successful people like Donald Trump, Richard Branson and so many more, to get a good understanding of how all these super-successful people think.

NLP

I enrolled in a course on NLP and did my masters, as this was touted as the ultimate for salespeople, but I found it to be extremely dangerous. It manipulated people to buy on a subconscious level. In the wrong hands, like anything, it could take advantage of people. This was against my principles.

Learning NLP is like learning the language of the mind. It is the study of excellent communication, physically and emotionally. You learn how to match and mirror people's speech, tonality, body language, etc., and how to mimic it back to them. The reason for this is people are most comfortable when dealing with what they know best. Imitating them without them knowing 'uncrosses their arms' and opens up their trust, subconsciously. It felt unethical to me.

Nevertheless, I learned how to become a chameleon in order to get what I wanted. Being in my 20s, I was still very immature and inexperienced in the game of life. As soon as my then sales manager pointed out to me how I was behaving, I realised I had to stop.

Now, I use the skills I learned in NLP training naturally, solely to make people feel comfortable by creating rapport. NLP is hypnotic subconscious communication. I have done a lot of self-hypnosis over the years and taken guided sessions to train my mind and my beliefs. These days I do meditation, to help me get out of my mind! When I take myself into a different place through meditation, it allows me to escape the outside world, all the noise, drama, chaos and stress. It helps me focus on my inside world of peace, solidarity, oneness and mind-body connection to the universe. A complete 360 degrees for sure.

Do I recommend NLP for sales? Yes, only if intentions are pure. If you want to learn the art of communication for yourself, then it is a great tool for interpersonal connection and self-re-programming.

ENERGY

I also started tapping into things like reiki, so I could understand energies more. Being energetic creatures, we can tell very quickly from our energies if we like or dislike somebody. Have you ever been in a room full of people and felt uncomfortable around somebody you have never met? Or have you ever felt somebody was looking at you for some reason?

That is the energy I am talking about. Very quickly I learned which people to avoid. If I did not pay attention to it at the beginning, it got me good and proper at the end. Reiki is used for healing, and it is a great tool for energetic self-regulation. It helps realign the chakras so we can live from a more balanced place.

SELLING THROUGH LEADERSHIP

It was fascinating that I was learning all this stuff so I could become a better salesperson. But there, I said it: a better salesperson, not a better person. My focus and intention in my younger days were all wrong. I used these tools for manipulation to some degree. I make no lie about it; it was all about simply getting more sales. That was my job and my sole focus.

Little did I know that people naturally gravitated towards me and my energy anyway. I can be extremely approachable, and I was always good at what I did. I am so grateful that in the coming years, I learned the art of selling through leadership, not force. That is the direction I want to see the world of sales take. Sales by leadership. When you are coming from that space, people buy from you because *they* want to. You are not selling to them because *you* want to. It is such a massive difference and energetically feels so much better for everyone.

To be a true salesperson via leadership, you must be able to emotionally regulate. Keep an even keel. Communicate at all levels. Be likeable and trustworthy and most importantly, have honesty and integrity as your mantra.

To do this, I absolutely recommend personal development, daily. These days with access via mobile phones, we can listen to amazing books and podcasts whenever we want. Make sure you set your day up to win, by setting up your mindset first. Listen for 20 to 30 minutes each morning. During the day, if you have any issues or challenges, have your own go-to method to help raise your vibration, which will raise your mental state. Do not take shit personally and have the tools to rebalance yourself when needed.

COMMUNICATION

The difference between a good salesperson and a great salesperson is communication. Internal and external. The more we learn about ourselves, the more we can balance out our energy and the more confident our behaviour becomes. The most important part of sales is listening. When you go through your personal development journey, you will absolutely become a better person, and this is the key to being a successful leader. Remember, selling is not about talking somebody into buying. Everybody hates that. A true sales leader is a matchmaker. That is when listening is key!

I have read so many books (which I list at the end of this book) and attended so many seminars. Truth is, if we look at things from a big picture perspective, our only objective in life is to grow and serve. When we invest more into ourselves, we become better versions of ourselves. By becoming better, we can serve more. The more we are of service, the more rewards will come our way. Why? Because money is simply a by-product of service.

THE EGO

Now I want to talk about the EGO.

Ahhh … the ego!

According to Wikipedia, the ego is, 'The part of the mind that mediates between the conscious and the unconscious and is responsible for reality testing and a sense of personal identity.'

There is nothing worse than cocky, arrogant, sleezy, egotistical salespeople! Personally, when anyone tells me they are a closer, it just makes me want to spew! I'm sure you know very well what I am talking about.

Ego and attitude in salespeople remind me of a great book titled *Sales Dogs* by Blair Singer originally published in June 2001.

Blair uses personality profiling to label salespeople into categories that resemble dogs' personalities or characteristics. It may seem funny comparing people to dogs, but it makes a lot of sense if you need to identify yourself as a typical style of salesperson. Here they are as described in this link: https://successresources.com/the-5-breeds-of-sales-dogs-which-one-are-you/

1. The Pitbull
The most aggressive and probably the most stereotyped salesperson of all is the Pit Bull. They will attack with a ferocity, aggression and tenacity that is both awe-inspiring and terrifying. All they need is a pant cuff to latch on to and they NEVER let go. Their intensity is rivalled only by their lack of fear. They are the classic thick–skinned, aggressive salesperson. Closing and objection handling is breakfast for this champion. The Pitbull's success comes from sheer power and fearlessness. They will make more calls, field more rejections, and keep on selling more than any other breed. It is the smash and grab game for these dudes ... CLASSIC!!

2. The Golden Retriever
Everyone's favourite is the Golden Retriever. The typical Retriever sells by providing extraordinary customer service and they will go to great lengths to grant favours for their customers. The wise Retriever is successful because they know that by continually taking care of prospects, clients and members of their team, customers will keep coming back and the referrals will flow. Long-term service is the key.

3. The Poodle
Poodles are highly intelligent and highly conscious of their appearance. They always look good and will never consider getting their paws dirty over chasing some stupid stick into

the river and into the mud. They know the latest trends and are incredibly well connected. In fact, they probably have the most extensive and exclusive network of any of the breeds!

4. The Chihuahuas

Chihuahuas are technical wizards. Their product knowledge and understanding of processes is astounding. When they have a point to be made, they are insistent about driving their point home. Don't ever get a Chihuahua started on a subject they are passionate about. They won't just talk, they will shout, scream, rant and rave a mile a minute. Prospects can only be amazed and impressed with the incredible exhibition of passion, emotion and technical detail. While the Chihuahua is not always the best lap dog, it's the breed you want on your team when digging up data and putting together vital presentations. With boundless energy, Chihuahuas can pull off all-nighters better than any other breed.

4. The Bassett Hound

The classic of all classics is the faithful Bassett Hound. This companion will stick by you through thick and thin. You may try to chase this dog away, yet it would always come back. When they sell, they have that distinctively humble approach that is designed to drive an arrow deep into your heart. If their pathetic look doesn't get you and begging doesn't work, beware! You may be about to experience plan B — the picture of their family and stories about having to pay for braces, bicycles and ballet classes! They will do anything to solicit your sympathy and their favourite word is "Please?" — "Please buy from me", or "Please give me an answer today".

I really love Blair's analogy of the different styles of salesperson personalities.

To me, ego is something that separates the 'men from the boys'. I have worked with humble salespeople and aggressive salespeople, misleading and deceptive salespeople, sleezy, technically correct salespeople... and the list goes on. The ego is all about creating a front and it highlights inefficiencies.

BUYER'S REMORSE

There is a massive difference between confidence and arrogance. A self-assured, confident, genuine salesperson will always win. They naturally sell with leadership. People want to buy from them because they are authentic. They see them, believe them and trust them. Because of that, the customer generally chooses to buy, which in most cases eliminates buyer's remorse.

Have you ever experienced buyer's remorse?

It normally comes as a by-product of buying something you did not want or need because somebody convinced you to, or it was an unexpected emotional purchase. It also comes from compulsive shoppers who spend money because they are looking for the instant fix or emotional pick-me-up, hoping it will make them feel better.

Companies know this and absolutely take advantage of people's emotional needs to generate more sales. And they make their salespeople prey on these customers. Society has changed and this is a whole other topic, possibly for another book. Nevertheless, this type of opportunistic selling disappoints me at times. How did the world become about taking advantage of people for money?

> I was talking to a colleague about an experience he had when he was first learning a new business venture for himself. The person 'teaching' him the ropes was demonstrating how to make easy money as a broker. His ego was obviously way out there. He told my colleague about a business owner who wanted to sell his business. He had only bought the business, a café, 12 months earlier. He had paid about $200k for it and spent some money building it up a little. The new café owner then told him he wanted to sell it for 1.2 million. Umm, excuse me?
>
> The broker said, 'No problem, I will list it at the price you want,' knowing too well it wasn't worth more than $300k. He gave the seller an invoice for $5k and mentioned to my colleague on the side, 'He has no hope of selling for this. It'll be on the market for six months, then he'll take it off. I'll then tell him what it's really worth and sign him up again for another $5k in listing fees. If we sell it, then that's a bonus!'
>
> How is that for unethical, egotistical sales tactics! Let's make a buck now and do it again later.
>
> Surely, the café owner knew the broker was taking advantage of him. We all know when we are being sold to. Personally, I hate it, and I cannot be sold to anymore. But I do like buying from people.

Have you heard the saying, 'a man convinced against their will is of the same opinion still'?

Imagine if a family member or one of your kids or close friends has been sold into something knowing it was the wrong thing to buy? It sucks.

Removing yourself from your head and following your heart or intuition eliminates the ego mind and allows you to operate from your higher self of knowing.

Misleading and misrepresenting to people for money is not the way to go.

Yes, in sales you can make a great living and be fuelled with internal passion to succeed. It's also a great platform to feed your ego mind and wallet from as money does not discriminate between good or bad people. Yet if you do it right, you become a world changer and a positive influencer. And somebody people always speak highly of.

You do need to have an ego, so don't get me wrong. It is just the intention that comes with it. 'Do unto others as you would have them do unto you' is a great way to sell from. That is coming from integrity and leadership values, and serving with the right intention.

If you are somebody who likes taking advantage of people for money, well there is a thing called the law of attraction. What you put out to the universe will always come back to you.

So, keep your ego in check. Nurture it and allow it to assist your growth from a positive standpoint instead of controlling you and your actions.

POSITIVE ATTITUDE AND AN ATTITUDE OF GRATITUDE

With sales, having a positive attitude is so important. Believing in the possibilities of a great outcome for all is where it begins.

Sales leaders operate from this space and it's evident in how they show up. Having an exceptional attitude will always set you apart from your competition. It will be one of the most memorable aspects of your relationship with people after the business has been completed. People will always remember how you made them feel, not the work you actually did for them.

A 'can-do' approach is refreshing when it comes from the space of selling with leadership, not simply from taking orders.

When I employed salespeople, I always looked for winners. It is an internal confidence that people have because they already know how to manage their emotional state, and they work on themselves constantly.

One other key aspect to having the right attitude that many would not consider is gratitude. I love this — there is no place for ego when operating from a state of gratitude.

Gratitude changes everything. Think about it. How many people are grateful for what they do? Where they work, who they meet, the lives they change by the service they supply? When operating from a space of gratitude, your energy is pure, which in turn means your intentions are also pure.

The energy and emotion of gratitude is the same as love. People pick up if you are a genuine person, and it makes connection so much greater. It is simply because again, you are coming from a space of service, not from wanting to get a sale. After all, it is the connection that builds the trust and the trust is what leads to business.

It reminds me of a post I saw one day on Facebook. Someone in a business group put up a whole spiel on how to get more clients by knowing your exact target market.

> It started off with, 'People don't invest when they don't see value in what you do.'
>
> Hmm ... I don't generally engage in this stuff but the comment got me thinking and I replied, 'People don't invest if they don't see value in YOU!'
>
> The response was, 'To an extent, but the conversation starts long before they even engage with you.'
>
> I disagreed, because what I was talking about was much more about the macro, the bigger picture. What that person was talking about was the micro, the smaller picture. They were missing a key component about human interaction and why we do business with people.

'Leadership is not a position or a title, it is an action and an example.'

DONALD MCGANNON

In sales, as a leader, your attitude is all about how you act and who you are. Having a positive attitude is not enough. You can be super-positive, but that does not mean you are a sales leader.

I have met so many people who are 'nice' and always 'positive', but would I follow them into the trenches? Probably not.

Would I follow someone who is prepared to roll up their sleeves and get their hands dirty while having an attitude of success? Always.

Being grateful, being positive, having a can-do attitude and leading from the front foot marks a great salesperson.

When it comes to gratitude it's very simple. Too often, people look at the end game and lose sight of the daily journey to reach that destination. It's great to be focused on the result but as Will Smith says, *'You don't set out to build a wall. You don't say "I'm going to build the biggest, baddest, greatest wall that's ever been built." You don't start there. You say "I'm gonna lay this brick as perfectly as a brick can be laid," and you do that every single day, and soon you have a wall.'*

Now that's attitude …

For the past decade, I have had a gratitude journal by my bed and each night before sleep, I enter everything that happened during the day that I am grateful for. Best part of this exercise is that I look for small things. I like doing my daily meditation, or thanking my body for allowing me to hit the gym (I'll touch on this next), or spending time with my kids, or the people I meet … It's very simple to list out 10 things each day that you're grateful for and it sets you up for allowing more things to be grateful for each day.

As soon as I learned the true concept of gratitude, it made my days so much bigger and better. I had so much more to look forward to and could take away positives even from the shittiest days in the field.

People overestimate what they can achieve in the short term and underestimate what they can achieve in the long term. Most people look at the prize and forget the journey of how to achieve it. If you are operating from an attitude of gratitude, you will find success and wins in the smallest of things. These small wins are all part of the progress needed to claim the prize. We can always take something positive away from all situations. Making that extra phone call, going beyond the call of duty to support a client. Helping fellow comrades on their path, it's all part of the bigger picture of being of service and it helps us stay grounded and humble, something most high-flyers have forgotten.

So grab a piece of paper and a pen and write down five or 10 things each day you're grateful for. Then watch how the universe opens up to bring more great things into your life to celebrate.

Doing this further instils the self-belief that you are great, that you do great things and that you have the courage to keep going.

The other journal I have by my bed is my creation journal. This is something super-cool for salespeople as we get to create what's in our mind and manifest it into our reality.

Did you know that thoughts are things? What does that have to do with attitude? Well, everything you see or have or want, at one time was a thought in somebody's mind. Look at inventors — it starts with a picture in their mind and then they set out to create it.

They give so much attention, energy and focus to it that eventually, it comes out of their mind, and into their physical reality.

Understanding that thoughts are actually things (just not manifested yet), think about this little phrase:

> 'What you think about, and thank about, you bring about!'
>
> **JOHN FREDERICK DEMARTINI**

If you live by this, it can change your whole reality.

Each night I write down what I want to create in my future. Meeting new people, networking, changing people's lives with my service, and so on.

I'm setting the intention and allowing my subconscious mind to manifest it into my reality.

This is the attitude of all successful people. You don't become successful by sheer luck. It is a strategic plan with constant visualisation, dedication and application. Your attitude needs to be as if you've already achieved everything you are working towards. You become very attractive to others when operating from this viewpoint.

HEALTHY BODY, HEALTHY MIND

Another thing I learned years ago was that a healthy body meant a healthy mind. Have you ever met obese people who are serious go-getters? They cannot be, as their thoughts are not full of energy. Now I am not saying you can't be successful as an obese person, I'm simply pointing out that if your body is healthy and strong, your mind will be too.

It's the same analogy as the saying, 'you are what you eat'. A healthy diet leads to optimum physical health. If your body is running efficiently, you will naturally be stronger in the mind.

Personally, I found that the harder I worked, the sicker I became. The more I pushed myself to create the result and the less I looked after myself, functioning optimally became impossible.

I was in my early 30s and I blew out to 95 kgs. I felt and looked horrible, and my personality changed. I was drinking a bottle of wine a night and smoking a packet of cigarettes a day, while eating rubbish food and not exercising. Looking at my attitude, how do you think I was showing up? Not great … I had mood swings, wasn't sleeping well and was irritable. My energy levels were low and the relationships around me were not great.

When I switched to becoming vegan, quitting the smokes and reducing the alcohol, my attitude naturally changed.

I was at the gym regularly. I got out every morning to walk our dogs and lost a bucket-load of weight. My confidence came back, my energy levels were through the roof and my attitude changed completely. Not long after that, I had my very first six-figure month!

Coincidence? Nope. Ego? Nope. Attitude? Yep!

Setting myself up to win by being grateful, planning my future, feeding my body with the right foods and enough water, sleeping well and constantly working on my mindset was the formula I found in creating longer-lasting success. It all starts with attitude.

Best part of this is that it is not rocket science and anyone can do it. It just takes commitment and dedication and most of all, accountability.

> 'Light yourself on fire with passion and people will come from miles to watch you burn.'
>
> **JOHN WESLEY**

Your attitude makes all the difference. Drop the ego, embrace your natural state and be your true authentic self.

Chapter 3

JUST BE YOU

'Authenticity is your most precious commodity as a leader.'

MARCUS BUCKINGHAM

BEING AUTHENTIC

Being authentic. Now there's a phrase that's absolutely being smashed these days!

I mentioned NLP in the previous chapter and how it has been used by people to improve communication. I also suggested it may be a great tool for sales, depending on the intention behind using it.

Personally, I think it is a positive thing to learn how to effectively communicate with people. However, through NLP the subconscious communication is done by working out how others communicate and then simply modelling that back to them. It makes them instantly feel comfortable dealing with you. That is why I am not a raving fan, as it is a form of mind manipulation.

See, being authentic is totally different. When you are your true authentic self, people 'buy' you. They believe you. They trust you. And from there, you create your own brand. Also, by being authentic, you do not need to pretend or hide behind what you are not. If you behave in a way that is not you, it is easy to get caught. From there, there is no return.

Look at the sales dog analogy and see if you fit into one of those types. If you do, own it. If you do not, stop trying to be something you are not. When being 100% yourself, you own it. Therein lies your personal power.

When you look at today's influencers, they are not trying to copy or imitate other people. They are being themselves, their own brand. That is why they have created their success. They are behaving from within, not being guided by the external.

It is important to learn the skills required to perform your job, but once you have the skills, it's imperative that your own natural flair and style is 100% all over the skills.

People who are true to themselves can sniff out imposters a mile away and are turned off instantly.

Let me give you a couple of examples of what could be inauthentic. I have seen two different real estate agents do their thing. One is a flamboyant male and the other an attractive female. They are both fighting for listings against their competitors and both work for a large national agency. Both are finding ways to establish their 'perceived' brand.

The male has absolutely smashed his brand by playing to his strengths by putting together what I thought was some of the best marketing ever on a property.

He portrayed himself as a woman, all dolled up, and pretended the house 'she' was selling was a resort and she was on holiday! It was a beautifully laid out place and had a great tropical feel to it. There was an outdoor bar overlooking the spa, and he got in an exotic bartender! The bartender was mixing drinks and rubbing his feet, all while he played a mini travel commercial to entice people to come and stay with him.

It was brilliant marketing, painted a great story, but was he being his true natural self?

The beautiful female agent had great sex appeal (I'll touch more on this soon). She created a video of herself in her listing. The property was a lovely house on water, a great lifestyle place. She showed footage of herself kayaking, swimming and jet skiing out in the water. Inside the house, she showed footage of herself cooking in the kitchen and relaxing on the deck while walking the pooch in the surrounding streets. It portrayed a great story of the lifestyle this house could offer. The image was set was for buyers to imagine themselves as that person. That is a great way to sell, it felt genuine. Key is to ensure you are being yourself when portraying the message for others. Not an actor.

Another example is a term called 'charlatan behaviour'. I once spoke to a financially successful business owner who came across as not too smart, dumbing himself down and indicating that his success was a bit of dumb luck. I asked him one day, 'Why do you portray yourself this way when in fact you are extremely intelligent?' His answer was, 'Because I want to relate to the "average" person, ultimately to make more sales.'

When you are portraying an image of yourself, own it. Be truthful and authentic. Only ever show yourself as you really are. Do not mislead people into thinking you are not what you represent. And worse still, don't put yourself in their shoes pretending to be them and thinking that is what they want. When you are a leader, you do not need to do that. What you are is naturally on display. Remember, just be yourself because everyone else is already taken.

This reminds me of another story.

> One day I got a message out of the blue from a 17-year-old I'd never met. He was working in a tele-sales business and had heard from another employee that I was one of the best salespeople who had ever worked there. Now, I had not been there for 14 years, but this kid messaged me wanting to ask questions on how he could be better.
>
> He did not know it, but he was showing leadership qualities and the best salespeople are also natural leaders. I liked that and decided to give the kid some of my time. He reminded me of the younger me, when I'd done exactly the same in my early days of sales. I'd sought out the best and wanted to learn directly from them. I wanted to know what made them tick and what skills they could help me learn to get the results I was after.
>
> This kid, let's call him Dave, wanted to run before he could walk or crawl. He went from salesperson to salesperson in that company looking for guidance. He kept changing his script and doing things differently each week to get the results he was after. That was a complete warning bell to me because once people start chopping and changing, they cannot build momentum and do not learn through their mistakes.

You cannot be something or someone you are not and get long-lasting results. It just does not work that way. I admired his tenacity and respected the lessons he must learn, but it cannot be forced. In one breath, he said he wanted to get better at his job, and in the next breath, he said he wanted to leave. Was he being authentic with himself? No.

SEX APPEAL

Now let us talk about sex appeal and slick looking dudes …

Are you a good, authentic salesperson if you need to dress in power suits, stylish high heels and lots of yummy perfume, cake on the makeup and bla, bla, bla? What about the guys in the Versace suits, polished shoes, slicked-back hair and fast sports cars? Nope.

Back in the day, they used to spruik that you needed to look the part. Looking the part has nothing to do with it. To me, that is ego driven, and you are representing a persona that is not you. If you would not wear certain clothes at home or on weekends, why wear them in a meeting? I think people are more comfortable when they are with people who look respectable and comfortable. A leader can look respectable and professional without needing to go out of their way to portray themselves as something they are not.

Yes, we are always being judged and we are always judging, so when you represent yourself in a certain way, ensure, first, that you feel good, and second, that you look good. Don't choose clothes that you think will make people respect you more. Be strong within yourself.

Dressing for sex appeal could be construed as taking advantage of others. Do not get me wrong, I love looking at beautiful people and I admire them most when they are naturally comfortable. Fake lips, tans, nails, eyelashes, boobs, hair extensions, caked on make-up, etc., is not, in my eyes, somebody being authentic to themselves.

Being authentic is the total package. It's about naturally being you in all ways. Your confidence will grow from within. Your energy is pure, and your attitude is certain. While we all have an image in our minds as to how we want people to see us, that's the ego again. Screw it. You want to be remembered for how you make people feel, for the service you provide, for your intentions being the best for the customer. Be yourself and buck the naysayers. You will never have a sleepless night and you will build a brand that starts getting repeat business, multiple repeat business and best of all, referral business when you are operating within your own integrity and authenticity.

> 'It is true that integrity alone won't make you a leader, but without integrity you will never be one.'
>
> **ZIG ZIGLAR**

According to Wikipedia, 'integrity is the practice of being honest and showing a consistent and uncompromising adherence to strong moral and ethical principles and values' — being authentic.

Hmm, unfortunately, it's something very few salespeople have. In my career, I can't begin to tell you how many salespeople I've met who are sleezy, desperate, downright disgusting liars.

Most salespeople tell their prospective buyers what they 'think' they want or need to hear to get the deal. Then they wonder why they are failing, just like the broker selling the business.

It really is simple. If you do not believe it yourself and you do not DO it yourself, you are out of alignment with your own internal integrity and you are not being 100% authentic.

When I look back at all the jobs and businesses I have had in my career, the reason I believe I succeeded at them was because of my moral compass. I never intended to rip people off or take advantage of them just for a sale. True, there were many times in my career where I found myself on the treadmill of doing what I needed to do in order to survive, but when I realised I was doing it, I knew it was time to leave the role. When I genuinely believed that what I was doing was good and it could make a difference, I excelled. When I lost that belief, when I went against my own internal values and integrity, I failed.

PRACTISE WHAT YOU PREACH

My first real commission-only direct sales job back in 2002 was in property investment seminars. I was 28 and had been unemployed for the few months leading up it. I had the mindset of one day being rich. The principles that company used reminded me of Robert Kiyosaki's *Rich Dad Poor Dad* series. Being exposed to personal development and success stories from very early on was most advantageous.

I believed at that time, the way to real wealth was in property. This company taught people how to buy property off the plan, with no deposit down, hold for a few years and sell at a handy profit or leverage it to acquire more property. We sold those courses and seminars for between $15,000 and $55,000 each! People paid it because we legitimately showed them on paper how very quickly, they would make that money back in their first transaction!

I was living in Melbourne, Australia at the time and the property market was going crazy. Some said that because of the work we did in educating people how to buy property, we drove the market up. Off-the-plan property sales were going through the roof and the market was so hot it became saturated. Yet I still saw it as a great way to get ahead.

INTEGRITY

When I suggest a great salesperson has integrity, I mean if you are going to preach it, you do it as well. Otherwise you're just another schmuck bullshitting your way through. While it took me a few months to gain traction with my sales, I was also learning how to acquire property myself. Within 18 months, my partner and I acquired three properties off the plan in prime inner-city locations to the value of $1.5 million at that time. Think my ego wasn't off the charts? We were holding a significant amount of property on paper and one of those properties had a four-year settlement.

I genuinely thought I was going to make my first million by the age of 33 simply by how fast the property prices were moving.

Did I believe $15k for educating people on how to do the same was worth it? Abso-fricken-lutely because I was proof that it could be done.

That was the key to my successful sales career. I was an actual participant in what I preached. I'd watch salespeople closing deals in that same company who never bought a property and had no intentions of doing so. To my mind, that just didn't add up.

However, even though things seemed amazing, I also saw how greed could destroy a company. The owners wanted to list the business on the stock exchange, make a shitload of money and sell out. The intentions of the company openly changed in front of my eyes and I saw it switch from being of service and making a difference in people's lives to ripping people off. We started having to 'close' people to get the numbers up. In order to list the company, it must be turning over a certain amount of profit to qualify.

It became all about sell, sell, sell — to the point where we were financing people to buy these $15k programs (which would take them four years to pay off), learning most of them had no means of actually following through on the education they were purchasing.

This just didn't feel right and very quickly, I started going from one of the best performers to one of the average performers. The company dissolved soon after, the directors were all out to get one another and I quit.

The moral of that is a great sales leader is somebody who can demonstrate, **do as I do**, not do as I say. When you are in that mode of operation, it is not selling. It is making a difference. That is why, as I mentioned earlier, it's important to align yourself with the right company.

How many drug reps take the drugs they sell?

> It reminds me of one morning I was out walking with my wife and we saw an older guy driving a Tesla car. My wife was shocked when she found out how expensive they were, but then I said, 'I wonder if for a living, he runs a toxic chemical company, or a green energy company.' She said, 'Well, buying a car like that is really about the environment,' and she wondered how deep his values and beliefs ran, such as whether he might be vegan, because the seats weren't leather.

Integrity runs deep. Rather than judging an innocent man here, I am merely using it as an example.

A similar thing happened when I was involved in my first business in the personal development industry. The BS detectors were going off like firecrackers in my gut, but my head wanted to believe it was true.

For years, I had been working towards what my true purpose in life was, what I was destined to be doing. I felt I was bound for greatness and for building something extra-special, but I just didn't know what I should be doing with my career. I spent years searching for it.

When I stumbled across that opportunity in personal development, although it felt wrong in my gut, my head took over. I was drawn initially to how much money could be made, not what I needed to do to make it. It seemed way too easy, and it didn't feel right. I was looking for the holes in it. I've always liked personal development and knew the changes that can come from applying the principles in one's life, and honestly I loved the idea of how much money I could make by being of service with life-changing products. But it's the old saying, 'if it's too good to be true, it generally is'. After my experience of fighting my ego for years and wanting things to be different, I believe that saying to be true.

The personal development/self-help industry has become one of the highest paying industries out there. So many bloody coaches now all think they are gurus, but they do not have their own houses in order and they are not living with integrity. It is all smoke and mirrors, as so many of the people involved do not live authentically what they preach. I have seen it first-hand.

Anyway, I worked that business for over seven years, three years part time alongside my full-time job and four years full time from home.

Now here is the interesting part. I had a never-give-in attitude and a NO plan B philosophy. I had invested so much time, energy and money into building this business that I wanted to see it through. I started the business in 2012 and was an up-and-coming leader in the organisation, winning a rising star award in 2013. I had my first $50,000 US profit month in 2015 and my first $100,000 US profit month in 2016! (That was $142,000 AU at the time.) And, I was a top three global income earner in 2015, 2016 and 2017.

I was a product of the product, immersing myself in all the personal development and buying into the belief that it really changed lives.

We travelled the world with our kids, taking them to seven countries, while on our own, we'd been to 11. I thought I had broken through the barrier and was set for a new level, except that after my record-breaking month of $100,000 US, I again learned that most of the people who had purchased programs from me would never use them and could not succeed in their own right. This ate at me for a while and subsequently I couldn't do it anymore.

How could I sell something to people for large sums of money when they wouldn't and couldn't use what they bought? Morally and ethically my integrity wouldn't allow it. My success came from being a leader, taking a stand for others and being the demonstration of what was possible through my own actions.

Having integrity is my super-gift. Doing things for the right reasons is a must in my eyes. If it is just about the dollar now, I'm out. I mentioned earlier that once you operate from a space of authentic service, success is simply a by-product.

'DO WHAT I DO'

The other thing that blows me away about salespeople is how many of them do not do what they say they are going to do. 'I'll call you back', 'I'll follow up on that for you', and so on.

My success came from dedication, vision, accountability and authenticity. If I said I was going to do something, I did it. As soon as you fail to follow through on your promise, your word becomes null and void, meaningless, and you lose credibility.

I love the quote by Mahatma Gandhi:

> 'Be the change that you wish to see in the world.'

There is a philosophy called **BE DO HAVE** which I learned years ago. Simply, it means, **BE** the person who **DO**es what they say they will do, and you will **HAVE** what you want. From a sales point of view, when operating from a leadership standpoint, if you live 100% by this principle, you will be a magnetic, pure, positive force to reckon with.

Chapter 4

WHAT DO YOU BELIEVE?

In my first business, I did a presentation at a Sydney event in front of 500+ entrepreneurs and business owners about belief. This was what I delivered on stage:

> 'Your **beliefs** become your thoughts.
> Your **thoughts** become your words.
> Your **words** become your actions.
> Your **actions** become habits.
> Your **habits** become your values.
> Your values become your **destiny**.'
>
> MAHATMA GANDHI

SELF-BELIEF

Self-belief is what separates a good salesperson from a great salesperson! A great salesperson has belief in themselves, belief in their abilities, belief in what they do or are representing and utmost belief in the outcome.

I've seen beginners at something absolutely smash it out of the park because when they first started, they had an underlying belief that they could do it. Because of this, their confidence and posture were strong.

Then there is the opposite, people who deep down know they don't have the belief and ultimately fail very quickly.

If I look back at my first career in commission sales, I had no belief in my abilities. In fact, I was petrified about selling $15,000 programs on property investments.

I was in my mid 20s, had never purchased a property before and never sold anything of such high value. I really thought, who will believe me or better still buy from me? I didn't have $15k to my name and at that stage in my life, would never have spent so much on any sort of course. Nowadays, it's so common for me I do not even raise an eyebrow.

In one of my early jobs, I quickly became the number one sales representative in an automotive company. Back then I was earning a whopping $35,000, and that was regardless of the result. I'm not sure why, but for whatever reason, I kept getting the best results month in, month out. Ironically when I started, I was the rookie and the least experienced of all reps on $26k while all the others were on $35k. It wasn't long before I was on equal wages with the rest. However, that job didn't have commission. I was capped, and I was secure. Well, that was until the business went into voluntary administration.

I became unemployed for nearly six months before I started the commission-only role. We had a drawback retainer system, like in real estate. I recall 13 or 15 of us starting at the same time and slowly as each day rolled by, more quit and never came back. It was too hard and too scary.

I was so far outside my comfort zone it was crazy. I had never done any form of consultative selling before. This was my first introduction to learning scripts. We had a one-hour-long presentation, almost like a rehearsal for a part in a mini-series. It was also my first job where after performing the presentation, I was required to close people on the spot. 'Don't let them leave without signing — press hard, three copies.' it was certainly a new world and one that was very foreign to me.

After two months, I was one of only three left from that first intake. I learned quickly that the game of commission sales was a constant hiring model. Not only was I sale-less, but I was also now in debt to them to the tune of over $6,000.

Sleepless nights were a new thing. I had no idea how to get myself out of this mess, other than to keep going. I had no idea how I was going to turn things around but even if I was going to be fired, I was determined to figure it out. I guess that is why they did not fire me.

I thought, 'Ok Adam, everything you have done so far, you have been at the top. So why can't this be the same?' I wanted to find out the difference between those around me who were succeeding and those who were not. It was simple. Skills, experience, positive attitude all equated to nothing if you did not have self-belief.

I had a dogged determination to always fight, and I had also come from successful outcomes, so deep down under all the uncertainty and fear there must have been a level of self-belief in there. Looking back at my sales career, I can honestly say that is where my belief grew from. I just never gave up.

Once I got my first sale in that job, which, mind you, took nearly three months, I was off and running. Over time, I went from being one of the youngest and most inexperienced, to one of the most successful. My self-confidence grew and so did my ego and attitude. The only thing that I believe separated me from many others was simply that I never gave up and I was always going to find a way to make it work. Again, no plan B.

There is a strong message in that. Too often people give up, and way too fast. It amazes me how people can think they are better at something or not good enough at something than someone else before they have even learned it.

They say it takes 10,000 hours before you are an expert in your field. So, how many people are experts in what they do? As a rule, very few because most humans are lazy and quit too easily. They want instant gratification and instant success, the easy way out, and if they can't get it, they move on. People have a sense of entitlement, as opposed to a deep-seated desire to earn it.

So how much is 10,000 hours? With a standard work week being 40 hours, it is 250 weeks, or 4.8 years.

When I was training people, I would see them come and go. Partly because they accepted a role that was not the right fit for their personality, and partly because they lacked belief and determination in mastering the job.

As I mentioned earlier in the book, people overestimate what they can achieve in the short term and underestimate what they can achieve in the long term. Think about it for a moment. Have you ever done this yourself? I'm sure you have.

Unfortunately, life does not work that way. Does a baby say, 'F#!k it, I'm giving up on running because I can't walk'? Nope. What happened to perseverance, determination, dedication? To me, the answer is simple: people like this lack self-belief.

When starting a role, it takes a good six months to have a solid grasp. That is why probation periods can last between three and six months. Give the job the chance it deserves. If you are outside of your comfort zone, even better! Life begins on the outside of that zone. If a company is prepared to invest in you, they obviously see something in you.

I've trained hundreds of salespeople and business owners over the years and without fail, I can tell quickly who will make it and who won't. Sometimes I'm surprised, but not too often. It always comes down to self-belief. It is crazy how many people are led more by fear of failure than by the possibility of future success. Yet sales is all about succeeding!

SELF-BELIEF AND SELF-WORTH

In many cases, self-belief is aligned with self-worth. I knew I was good at what I had done in the past, and in order to get better, I knew it was time to start working on myself. Hence, my passion for personal development arose. Mindset is key. I spoke about that before. Without a great mindset, you really have nothing.

Some people have it naturally, others work on themselves to create it. It is the 'working on oneself' that is the key. Personal and professional development. The average person who goes to university will pay over $50,000 for their education and in most cases, never end up using the qualification. Yet in sales, people rarely invest in their education. Personally, I have invested hundreds of thousands in my own on-the-job training and education.

Our pay is equivalent to our worth. So, the more skilled and experienced you become, and the more you fail your way to success, the greater the results will be for you and the company.

I mentioned in another chapter to align yourself with a product or service you would personally consume or support. By doing so, you create belief in yourself. Then look at the people there. Surround yourself with those who are succeeding and look at who they are as people first. Their attitudes, their mindset and experience. Interview them. Listen to their answers. Not the words, their body language. Feel their passion and see if you resonate with it. See how their attitude and personalities come across and make you feel. Look within yourself to see if you too can believe in it.

Then look at the company. Its values, service, vision. Is it something you can believe in? How do the end users feel? Then, finally, can you see yourself adding value by being of service? If you can, do you see yourself succeeding? If the answer is 'yes', then GO FOR IT!

WHAT DO YOU BELIEVE?

Sales is not just a career, it's a way of life. If you look at all those who have succeeded in their sales careers, you will notice they are the same people who also tend to succeed in life. Their self-belief is extended to all areas, especially when they live authentically.

Life is a journey of constant ups and downs. There are times when we are winning and times when we are losing. One thing is for sure: how you show up in your work is a direct reflection of how you show up in your life.

Our ups and downs in life contain lessons for us to learn and grow from. Look at the beaches. Every day the sun rises and the tides come in, and every day the sun sets and the tides go out. Yet each day the landscape is different. Having a never-give-in, never-give-up attitude is a true test of one's character.

> When I used to play cricket, my team was in the grand final and the game was in the balance. I had rolled my ankle but was still on the ground and doing my best on the boundary line. We only needed a few more wickets to win the match and there were only around 10 overs left to bowl. A ball was skied right to me, and I ran (well, hobbled) in a bid to catch it. It was a regulation catch, but I got nervous because I knew what the stakes were — winning the match was on this catch. All I heard were the echoes of voices from the boundary line as the anticipation built, and I buckled and dropped the ball.
>
> I probably should not have been out there to begin with, but I kept going.
>
> Instead of giving up, I went back to my position, ready for the next delivery, and the bowler went back to his position to start his run-up again.

Luckily, we got that wicket two overs later and it was the one we needed. We all had a sense of victory and the energy levels went right up. As a team, we were right behind one another. We wanted that win so badly that we never gave up and ultimately won.

It was one of the best experiences in my life and it taught me that despite the odds, despite our chances, if we keep showing up with the right attitude and dedication, we could make it happen. And we did.

In many ways, sport is no different from business. I've always had a sports mindset when playing at work and I think it's definitely held me in good stead. Coupled with the extensive personal development I am doing, I understand that nothing lasts.

In sales we have great runs. When a salesperson is on fire, they can do no wrong. Momentum is escalating and sales opportunities just keep falling into their lap. Whatever is going on for them shows that they are in absolute flow. I always tell them to bottle it! I ask them to record themselves. To keep an eye on their attitude, their energy levels and what they are doing on a day-to-day basis. When you are having a dog of a time and feel as if your back is against the wall, you can easily go back and look at what you were doing when things were going right.

It takes time to build back up to it and to understand that within the bad times there are more growth and learnings to make you a better person and subsequently a better salesperson. But the hard times often make people want to quit.

Once that idea hits their mind, it is almost game over.

At that point you must go back to why you are here and why you do what you do. It's imperative that you take the focus off yourself and refocus on your 'why' and 'what'. You simply must want it more than the person next to you.

This is the part of sales where people may say, 'Fake it till you make it.' My advice is never to fake it. Never pretend to be something you are not. When I speak about being authentic and holding yourself accountable with your integrity, faking it never comes into play.

Remember, people want to buy from people they like, believe and trust. If you are showing up fake at work, how are you showing up to people in life? I loathe that saying and much prefer to teach people to act 'as if' instead. Acting 'as if' is so much more powerful. Despite your current circumstances, you can believe in and behave how you want things to turn out instead.

I love the scene in *Rocky V* when Rocky is talking to his son about how life beats you to the ground and how you have to keep moving forward, keep getting up. Take all the beatings and keep moving on. That is winning! Now, I'm not saying that sales will beat you to the ground, but I am saying that each day and week, each month, we are constantly building. There will be times of flow and times of force. The key to being a great salesperson, one who stands up with leadership, is that no matter how you are feeling, no matter how full your pipeline is and no matter how much activity you have on, you keep showing up and giving it your best. That is acting 'as if' and that is you coming from a space of knowing it will all turn around.

Sales can be the most fulfilling career ever if treated like the game of life. You'll enjoy the ebbs as well as the flows of your journey. You may start off somewhere like I did, and correct your course over time until you find your true calling. Just do not give up on yourself and always make sure you are coming from a higher viewpoint with the right intentions to do good.

From there, the results will take care of themselves, especially if you are operating from a space of gratitude. So many salespeople operate from a space of expectation and entitlement. If you look at the journey you're going through with reading this book, hopefully some 'aha' moments have come up for you. I am sincerely grateful that you are reading this!

Chapter 5

CREATE YOUR RESULTS BY DESIGN

'A goal is a dream with a deadline.'

NAPOLEON HILL

I mentioned earlier that people are easily scared off by their fear of failure (hello, it's your ego talking) versus their drive to succeed, taking their future possibilities into account. People spend too much time wanting the instant reward or quick fix as opposed to working strategically towards it.

When you take on an opportunity, do you look at the perks and what the opportunity offers you? Your pay, conditions, expectations of role and your position, etc.? That short-term vision ultimately leads to failure because all you are setting yourself up for is the short term! How could you possibly succeed if that is your attitude?

CLEAR VISION AND GOALS

Thoughts are things. What we think about and thank about, we bring about. Every single thing we see in our physical world at one point started with someone's thought. The average person thinks 70,000 thoughts a day. Most are negative. Through meditation and strategic visioning, I learned how to train my mind to focus more on what I wanted to create in my life. One thing I was always good at was seeing the future. I always had a clear vision of where I wanted to take things. Yes, I was ambitious, yes, I wanted to climb the ladder and yes, I always wanted to succeed.

Having a clear vision with goals and focusing more on what we want to create versus what we have not yet achieved is important in a strong, long-lasting sales career.

INTENTIONS MATTER

What I learned along the way was the importance of setting the intention for what I wanted to achieve.

When I find an opportunity, I always look at what I can bring to the table. I assess my strengths and weaknesses, and what the opportunity can provide me in the future. Everything is part of my evolution and growth. Sales is a perfect extension of fostering that growth. It is tangible and through it, I can see it quickly play out from the effort I put in. I want to serve. I want to make a difference. I want to be successful at it and as a by-product, earn a great living and have a great life! I plan each day towards that ultimate vision.

Every self-help book I read, every audio book or podcast I listen to, every seminar I attend, every stimulating conversation I have, they all help towards making me a better person first, a better leader next. Forever improving my skills is a simple extension of that.

I mentioned before that I always gravitated towards the leaders and the most successful, like a sponge, to learn and leverage from them. The sign of great leadership is taking what you learn and passing it on to others. I always took those below me and helped them rise and grow with me. It is so much better doing it with others. Seems strange to hear that in a sales and business environment, right? Wrong. I know that for my growth and learning to continue, I must be able to teach it to somebody else. In business though it's the opposite because people are afraid you will take their spot, so they push you down. In Australia, it is called 'tall poppy syndrome'. Keep kicking them down because we want to be on top.

To be a great salesperson or business owner, I learned it is not about me, it is about everyone else.

My vision for success in any of my roles has been to create a group of leaders around me, all striving for a similar result. Together we can create so much more! I know my desired outcomes and I set to work to create them.

There are a few different types of salespeople, including those on salary earning a wage, and those on commission or profit share. The latter are like business owners, wanting to get the most out of their efforts and striving for more, like me.

When I speak to most salespeople who are ambitious and strive for more, they are clear on their outcomes, their goals and generally they are bigger picture thinkers.

Like me, each year they set themselves a goal of how much money they want to earn. $100k, $250k, $500k, $1M etc.

A goal is simply an idea of the future or the desired result that a person or a group of people envision, plan and commit to achieve. Now here is something fascinating. Why don't most goals set by people ever get achieved? Like a new year's resolution?

FLAWED GOAL SETTING

This took me a long time to work out, so here it is … GOAL SETTING IS FLAWED. Why? Because it comes from the left-side brain, the ego mind. The left side of the brain is said to control logic and analysis, while the right side controls creativity and intuition.

When tapping into the left side, we are setting goals based on external influences, or on what society tells us. These include goals we set based on competition or comparison. For example, you see somebody driving a car or going on a holiday or wearing a particular brand of clothing or doing something that you want, so you decide you want it too.

In that moment you are comparing yourself to others and taking other people's goals on board. Why don't you ever achieve them? BECAUSE THEY ARE NOT TRULY YOURS!

In order to actually achieve a goal, you must be clear on what YOU want, for YOU and only YOU. Clarity comes from spending time working out what is important to you on the inside, and what each goal means to you and why you really want it.

Each year, and throughout the year, I set up a vision board with pictures. I ask myself, what do I want to achieve this year? What is going to bring me joy? What is going to give my work meaning, so I show up and perform to the best of my abilities and want to be better?

All the money in the world means nothing next to my family. Giving my family experiences and opportunities to follow their dreams is a massive driver for me. Plus, I do like my toys. What excites me is knowing, for example, that I will be putting a swimming pool in our back yard, landscaping the gardens and extending the house. I love travel. Taking our kids around the world exploring is something super-special. These are great goals and the reason I get out of bed to perform each day. I love cars, and want a jet ski, a motorcycle, etc. It all costs money and I know exactly how much I want (notice I said 'want', not 'need') to create this.

WANT vs NEED

Let me touch on that for a moment. How do you feel when you say to yourself, 'I want that', compared to 'I need that'?

The energy is very different.

A leader wants, a manager needs.

Because the energy is different, wanting something allows it to flow into your life more effortlessly. If your goals are based around what you want vs what you need, then the likelihood of achieving them is much greater.

Now back to goal setting.

As above, I think it is great to get clear on what you want to create. Being specific is good. Once you understand the motivation, you can assign values to it, like $200k, $300k, $500k …

Let's say I select my number for the year as $500k.

I then ask myself some deep questions to meditate on and see if this is true for me. If it aligns with my gut and intuition. To achieve my goals, I need my heart to lead, not my head. How many salespeople lead with their hearts? Not many … but only then are you in true alignment.

How many different types of goal-setting techniques have you heard of? For shits and giggles, let's look at a common one. SMART goals. SMART stands for Specific, Measurable, Attainable, Realistic and Timely.

Hmm — let's break this down.

Specific: Good, but not from your head space. Head goals are just head fucks! Go with your heart-centred goals every time. It will increase your chances a hundredfold because there is emotion or feeling attached to it!

Measurable: What does that mean? To me, it is a logical attainment. Testing and measuring are good, in the sense that you do need to know if you are on the right path and if you are not, how to correct your course to get back on the right path.

Attainable: Hmmm, this one I do NOT agree with. I would much rather aim for the moon and hit the stars, as opposed to aiming for the sky and hitting the ground!

When we say attainable, in many cases, we are limiting ourselves, not extending ourselves. Our human nature is to expand and grow, not shrink and die. So, if it's a new car, why not aim for something you truly want, instead of settling for something you can only just afford or are prepared to settle for?

Realistic: Now WTF is that? Realistic compared to what and according to whom? The word realistic in an unrealistic world makes no sense. Realistic in my mind is again lowering one's expectations. Now I do agree that if your identity is not in line with your goals, you will fail for sure. So perhaps, this should be identity instead of realistic. Our identity is our DNA. It is what drives us from within. Our values, our morals, our integrity, our purpose, our soul. Everybody is different because of their identity. When setting goals, you must know yourself and be true to yourself. When you work from that space, yes again, you are in alignment and yes again, you have a higher chance to succeed.

Timely: Now here is the big one. Time. Time is the only thing in life we have zero control over. Time is a manmade measurement and all I know is that with belief that something will eventuate, it will in its own divine time. Strategically yes, I understand why a time limit is used, but it is totally out of our hands. It is however good to put a time frame on a goal, although please remember that it is never set in concrete and can (and usually will) be altered. The best part of setting a time frame is that it can keep you accountable to stay on task, and it can also help you prioritise what is most important. That way you can give more energy to completing the task first.

MAKING GOAL SETTING WORK

The main reason goals don't work for people is that the subconscious mind can't go so far into the future. Most people quit early because they can't see themselves reaching their goal. So, if you only focus on the result, you will fail. Once you are clear on your end goal, it is important to break it down into medium and short-term objectives. That then makes it feel more attainable and therefore you are more likely to keep on track because you can almost touch it!

The best way to do this is to break your year up. You've got your end goal in mind and that's the place to operate from. All your future decisions must be in line with the end goal, but you need to break it down into smaller pieces. I would do this by having a six-month goal, and a three-month goal, then a monthly goal and a weekly goal. Each is a natural extension broken down into bite-size chunks to achieve the end goal.

Best way to do this is to operate with a 90-day game plan. We do this because three months is a good amount of time to create momentum and to measure activity and performance when it comes to achieving your targets.

Now, we all have exactly the same amount of time in a day, 24 hours. How you use that time will determine the velocity at which you achieve your set goals. If I had a goal to save $100k in six months and it took me 12, would I care? Nope! That is because the goal is the $100k, not the time it takes to get it.

Be clear on this and remove any unnecessary pressure to make it happen. That way you give yourself the best possible chance of achieving it!

Chapter 6

HOW CAN I BE OF SERVICE?

'Earn your success based on service to others, not at the expense of others.'

H. JACKSON BROWN JR

Righto ... time for the nitty-gritty of value exchange!

Before we can get into profit, we must understand what money is. It's a manmade symbol or medium of exchange to facilitate transactions. In other words, it is just a 'thing' of perceived value as a replacement for goods or services.

The industrial age emphasised work for money. People then put value on the money they received instead of what they were doing, and unfortunately their self-worth diminished because they valued themselves as highly or lowly as the symbolic gesture received from their efforts. You will only get paid 'X' amount and if you do not like it, I will pay somebody else to do it. The greatest fear of all time is the thought of missing out, which becomes the reason they do it.

That, my friends, is slavery 101. We will tell you what you are worth, you will accept it, and away you go to earn it.

Money, however, is much more than that. It is pure energy. It flows like energy from hand to hand. As mentioned earlier, it does not discriminate between good or bad people. It also does not judge. Did you know that $13 trillion circulates around the planet each day, moving from account to account, and nobody even sees its transference? We put so much emphasis on what money is, the need for it, the want for it and the status of having it, because it makes us think we are better or more powerful or more successful than another.

Bob Proctor sums up money in an interesting way. He says money is just as important as oxygen. Without it, you will die. Hmmm, I see plenty of happy people in third-world countries who don't have it and who are alive and happy. Would they like to have a better standard of living? Yes, of course they would, but how much money do you need for a better standard of living? It gets to a point that no matter how much money you have, it really is all about your values as a human being. Look at Warren Buffett. He is the most successful investor ever to live. His company Berkshire Hathaway is one of the greatest stocks on the stock market to buy, yet if you watch the documentary about his life, *Becoming Warren Buffett*, you will see he lives a humble and modest life, even with billions of dollars.

Warren says, '*Price is what you pay. Value is what you get.*'

So, when I see organisations that are all about KPIs and bottom line and increasing profits and cutting costs, they have lost the true intrinsic value of the energetic exchange that comes naturally through the value of service.

They force their salespeople to sell, sell, sell.

Close the deal, find more prospects, close more deals.

Most of these salespeople get paid shit money, have to work long hours and are pressured to perform out of the fear of losing their jobs, so they in turn have to pressure others to buy. It's a vicious cycle and companies continually keep finding new people to carry out the role for them.

How do you feel when you know this is happening to you? Nobody likes being on the receiving end of it. I certainly don't!

It really is nothing more than greed. Worse still, when is enough, enough? It never is ...

Yet in the corporate world, this is what it has become. The boss is happy because he's made more money, the salespeople are relieved that they get close to hitting their targets and are allowed to keep their jobs, but the end user feels awful. Will they ever recommend people to you or your company or repeat buy? Nope, never! So it's off to the market again to find some fresh meat.

Let's take the example of the typical real estate agent. Their sole job is to get the best price for the owner who is selling. They constantly ask prospective buyers if they are prepared to put an offer down. They get the offers, take them back to the owner and start negotiating. Instead of trying to get the price the owner wants, they persuade the owner to decrease their pricing to match the market. The buyer has all the power; the agent just wants the sale so they can move on. They want the deal done. BUT ... the attitude of the agent won't get them any more business because their intentions are all wrong. They have made it about themselves, but they turn it around so the sellers think they got a good price. The buyers will never sell through them because they know how easily they can be squeezed, and the owners will never refer others to them because deep down, they don't believe they did a good job.

In relation to salespeople keeping their jobs, I know this all too well. When I was on menial wages, there was no incentive to perform other than the fear of losing my job. Age-old motivation to make me perform because I was scared.

Then I moved into the world of direct sales, and that world is sink or swim. No sell, no eat … I was forced to learn a completely different way of selling. I became an animal. I will always remember somebody I once worked with labelling me 'the closer'. 'Give that lead to Adam, he will close them.'

At the time I thought, 'YEH, this is cool! I'm a legend!' Fucking ego of a 25-year-old … I was getting off on it for ages. In the end, it became sickening. We started work at 8 am, finished at 9.30 pm and I was exhausted. But the thrill of the deal, which was worth between $800 and $2,000 in commissions, kept sucking me in.

Everything in life became about saying to my partner, 'It's only one more deal.' My life was about deals. I'll never forget, I was in Hobart in a hotel closing people on $50,000 property mentoring programs. One guy, his name was David, was all excited about the program we were selling, and he said to me, 'Adam, I lost my farm, my marriage and all our money. I am driving taxis to make ends meet and I will borrow that money from my sister to get started.' It was all her life savings ...

I knew in my heart of hearts it was wrong to sell to him and take his money. I knew he didn't have the financial means or support to follow through on the program he wanted to buy. I called my company director to explain my moral dilemma and she said, 'Take his money, do the deal.'

At that moment I was out! I learned something about greed and money that day that shaped my future forever.

Do the deal, take the money ... what is that? Do we not have a duty of care? Nope — not when it is all about getting the sale and the bottom line. Not when it is about getting the money and we will deal with it later.

I spent two decades doing phone sales for different industries: stock market advisory services, advertising, sponsorship, online businesses ... it was all the same. Direct sales is all about getting the deal and making money. I even bought into the life of thinking making money was our birthright. I found myself at one point in the personal development industry regularly making a profit of $45,000 from people, when I knew all too well they would not succeed at what they were endeavouring to do.

All was supposedly okay because I was told by my superiors, 'It is their decision to buy, not yours.' Just like my boss in stock market advisory days saying to me, 'Adam, either you take that person's money or someone else will.' It felt wrong to me. Zero integrity, all profit — but that is traditional sales and traditional business.

That is why I say, if you need to close people in order to get the deal, you shouldn't be in business because you don't have a reputable business or product that genuinely provides a real service.

Here is where intention and integrity come into play.

If your intention is to just get sales, as a salesperson, you will always be chasing and never fulfilled. Personally, I love being creative in my prospecting with how I can meet the right people. If your intention is to serve and be of service, and to make a difference while genuinely believing in helping others, not only will you survive in business, you will also thrive and be a money magnet!

People will refer others to you, people will repeat buy from you, people will become raving fans.

You can charge what you like because people know what they are getting from YOU. If you value yourself and value your products and value your service, so will they.

One of the most successful businesspeople in Australia is Mark Bouris, the founder of Wizard Home Loans, the second-largest mortgage broking business in the country. He honestly believed in helping people save money on their biggest investments. He felt that the more he could help them save, the faster they could pay off their homes and the sooner they could get in front financially.

Put yourself in the shoes of the buyer. Would you rather be talked into buying something, or genuinely want to buy from someone because you felt good and you knew the salesperson had your best interests at heart? When putting yourself in the buyer's shoes, how you feel is everything.

A lot of profit can be made and when it's a genuine win-win, people prefer to buy, rather than being sold to.

Fall in love with your clients, not the sale. You must set higher standards and think differently to create a different result. Become passionate about what you are doing and why you're doing it and get inspiration from every client you serve.

Ask yourself, would you prefer to be a sales leader operating from a place of integrity with values, or would you prefer to be a sales animal, on the hunt and closing people? I know which I prefer …

Chapter 7

GET INTO BED WITH THE RIGHT COMPANY

'Do what you love
and the money will follow.'

MARSHA SINETAR

In sales, most people simply do not cut it. That is because people find themselves just looking on the job sites for a position, not a career. Searching for something that pays okay (limiting one's self-worth) that meets their lower-level requirements. There is no passion, no excitement, no purpose or soul connection, no meaning or energetical alignment. Yet people still wonder why they do not succeed at it.

They find themselves going from job to job with the same mindset and attitude, getting zero job satisfaction. It is a trap, a long and windy road with lots of pit stops along the way, and no destination other than resentment, regret and disappointment. Also, mostly, for the privilege they're capped at a whopping $25p/h or $50k per annum. Hardly worth getting out of bed for!

Many of these salespeople can be 'good' at their jobs by simply learning enough skills to get by. But is that enough for either party? Nope! From the employer's point of view, it takes a lot of time, energy, effort and money to get someone up and going. So, you can understand their disappointment when it doesn't work out after all their efforts to get it right.

From a salesperson's perspective, if you are great at your craft, you could be in the top 5% of highest earners in the world. These people earn $500k+ a year and that's simply because they love what they do and are great at it. They love the company they work with. Their values are in line with the company's and there is genuine co-creation. They love the products they sell, and they are super-passionate about WHY they do it. These people are working with purpose. They are making a difference and they are connected to their inner ambition.

Naturally, they have become experts in their associated fields and are no doubt highly regarded and respected members of the organisation. There is a key difference between them and the standard worker: they are fully aligned and living on purpose. Their work is part of who they are — their integrity, their vision, their ethos and their values, and they are making a difference.

STEP ONE

Finding a company that is in alignment with you is the first step. Treating it just as a job will not work. I mentioned co-creation. What if you worked for an organisation whose values, morals, ethos, ethics and integrity matched yours? Instantly, you would have a great level of respect for them and they for you!

As mentioned already, sales is the lifeline of every business. Would you want to invest your time and energies into a company whose sole purpose was for themselves and how much they could make from your work? Would that motivate you to perform? Nope! I look at it from the point of view that we are in business together.

Looking for forward-thinking businesses to align with is the step that is missing for most salespeople. When I go to work with somebody, it is an absolute win-win basis. As a co-creator I am happy to set out to achieve the company goals if they are in line with my goals. We both get a fair portion of the profit share. I understand the companies are taking on all the financial risk. My risk is my time, which does not have the same skin in the game. So, if my income is based on a fair return of the profit, that excites me. I then do not feel as if I am being ripped off, so I approach the task or job from a completely different standpoint.

Under these circumstances, if ever I feel any form of emotional burden, resentment or victimisation — the 'poor me' syndrome — then I know I am out of alignment with myself. It has nothing to do with the company I am aligned with; it is simply self-sabotage. If my intentions are not pure, I know I am in it for the wrong reasons. Interestingly, that would probably be the case for over 80% of the sales workforce. Companies know that too and are always on the lookout for the salesperson's mindset and attitude because they cannot afford to allow this to infiltrate their organisation. That's probably why many have the attitude that anyone is replaceable.

STEP TWO

Once there is pure alignment, we can focus on step two!

The question to ask is, How can I be of service to you, the customer?

We can all smell a salesperson a mile away. When the phone rings, we immediately know when somebody is trying to 'sell us'. As soon as we walk into a store, we notice when a salesperson is all over us. Then when we do decide to buy, there's a constant upsell. Like we really need that!

What I am talking about is having the right intention and ethics when we supply a product or service. We want to approach it the right way by giving the customer the space to make their own buying decisions.

When you work alongside a company whose intentions are for the greater good, to serve first, to offer high levels of customer focus and to make a positive difference to the industry, and that company is also 'in business' with all their staff, then jackpot — you're really winning!

People perform at much higher levels and create significantly greater results when they feel part of something and know their efforts are genuinely appreciated. They do not need to push or force. They act with integrity and honour, wanting only to do the best thing for the customer.

Companies interview their salespeople, and salespeople should also interview the company. It really does go both ways.

Discovering your passions is simple — and that is the best place to start. Once, when I was unemployed, I put pen to paper and wrote down all the things I was interested in. Sports, business, personal interests, etc., things that I could easily talk about. Then I looked for companies in those industries whose products I personally bought. After that, I researched their values and mission statements and looked for people who worked there to pick their brains.

I ended up with a list of around 100 businesses that I could have easily worked for and I rang them one by one, enquiring about sales roles. Nobody was directly recruiting, but it set in motion to the universe my desire to be proactive in my search for creating opportunities. I never got to work for any of those companies, and ultimately chose a quite different path. I went for the money, pure and simple. I worked my arse off selling my soul year after year for companies I couldn't stand, with products that made zero difference to people's lives. Ultimately, I hated myself and hated what I had to do to make money in order to provide for my family. I was never in alignment at a core level, and it wore me down to burnout, time after time. That is why I clearly know the difference. At the same time, I have no regrets, as I understand everything happens for a reason and now, I can simply point it out to you.

The other thing that is important when choosing a company to align yourself with (notice I said, 'align yourself with', not 'work for') is one that is prepared to invest in YOU.

You will become a great asset to the company. Your personal reputation will make you and the company extraordinarily successful over long periods of time if your foundations are set up correctly.

Coming from a primarily direct sales background, I know that the attitude of sink or swim is rife. When you begin, they say here you go, give you a little bit of information and expect you to hit the ground running. If you don't succeed, that's fine, they will advertise again. They keep recruiting until they eventually find someone who might succeed, then they invest a little bit of time into them. The attitude is that if you throw enough shit on the wall, some will eventually stick.

I learned the hard way. If it is to be, it is up to me. I aligned myself with those who were creating success within each organisation and tried to copy what they did. Over time, it became abundantly clear that sink or swim was not the way to go for either party.

When you're looking for the right company to align yourself with, choose one that has a medium-term vision for you. A company that values its co-workers and invests in them. I prefer to work alongside an organisation that understands that my success is their success, and wants to mentor, train and coach me to become the best. Aligning with a company that wants you to succeed and will do their bit to ensure that happens is critical for mutual success.

If your attitude is the same as such a company's, then there is real synergy and a total win-win. Loving the industry, the company, the products, the service, the support and the leadership, and knowing you can make a difference well beyond your direct job to all the clients, is the best!

If the onus is on you to rise to the top, the company knows it will go through staff at a high rate. This builds resilience and it creates determination, but it is not supportive. There is no 'I' in the word 'team'. Through collaboration, we can do so much more than any one individual can.

Companies that recognise you as their greatest asset and that reward you for your time, effort, energy and work experience have greater synergy and a much bigger vision than those that don't.

Imagine how it would feel if your manager or hierarchy cared about you, instead of using you to make them more money.

How do you feel when you know you are being appreciated and heard and respected for your efforts and contribution? How does this compare to how you feel when you are told what to do, right or wrong, and made to work extremely hard to achieve ridiculous targets to receive commission, or even to keep your job?

I know that people always perform better when they are heard and appreciated. They contribute more, they want to achieve more, they go over and above the call of duty to do more. It's never about what they earn; it's always about how good they feel because they are valued and know they are doing good.

Slavery died with the industrial age. And to my mind, so did this method of management/dictatorship.

If companies continue to push their staff with KPIs, budgets, higher targets and fewer rewards, they will continue to have a high attrition rate and lose thousands of dollars a year in the indirect costs of high staff turnover. If instead they showed genuine appreciation for their staff, taking the time to learn about their families and personal interests, they would have a much higher retention rate, saving thousands of dollars each year and providing a harmonised and energised working environment.

Because they do not, chances are they will only ever rehire the same types of people. Why? Because it is always the same types of people, at the same stages in their lives and careers that apply for the same types of roles. It always comes back to their self-worth. Generally, such a person's self-worth is so low, they are subconsciously happy being treated like crap and that is why they never strive for more. I have seen people do the same thing for years, content within their little bubble.

When I was younger, I once worked in a retail environment. Crappy pay, crappy hours, crappy piddly little jobs like stacking shelves, washing floors, standing all day serving and asking permission to go to the toilet. The age-old adage of the customer always being right left me open to regularly receiving some sort of verbal abuse. And for that, I needed to learn how to smile — *#notwinning*!

Whatever happened to self-worth, and when did it become okay for people to be treated so poorly? Here is a better question. Why on earth do people tolerate it!

This is never good for performance, workplace stability, morale or harmony. From the company's perspective, people do not care about the business and will only ever do the bare essentials in order not to get fired. I totally fail to see how this can benefit the business, or the salesperson. It sure as hell can be seen a mile away by the customer!

How about this ...

What if companies you worked with saw you as a person, not just an employee? What if the company owners thanked you — genuinely thanked you?

And what if you as the owner or manager treated them as if they were your business partner instead of your worker. What type of response do you think you would get from them? Do you think they would be excited to turn up each day for work? Not take sickies. Perform their jobs to the best of their ability because they had a vested interest? What do you think their self-worth would look like then?

Imagine an environment where success was celebrated from above to below and vice versa. A place where everyone knew their role for the organisation to succeed, and was rewarded accordingly. That is oneness. Professional sporting teams only win the last dance because of this. Sure, there will often be a Michael Jordon who gets all the accolades, trophies and massive pays, and there will always be a player who offers their best but who doesn't get the same heroic status. Yet each one of the team needs the other to be the best, to win each game.

By taking an interest in each individual and running the business accordingly, instead of via a hierarchy, the business will produce results beyond everyone's wildest dreams.

I know personally that if a business genuinely cares about me and my life/family, I will go over and above for them — BIG TIME. Nothing would ever be too much because I know they want me. Basic 'Human 101'. This is so very different from using me. Quite different from someone saying, 'I'm paying you to do that.' The energy around both is astronomical. It is no surprise that forward-thinking companies that employ people as 'co-business owners' instead of staff go further. Ideas for improvements are given willingly. Tasks are carried out freely and the positive environment of the workplace is infectious.

Imagine a business that operates like that! Let me be the first!

People would come in droves because they'd want to be part of it. Not just for the money, but because of how they feel when they are there. Then it could be taken to the next level. What if the business also gave back? What if they helped support their partners' natural growth towards becoming better people?

What I have come to learn is that life, business, relationships, wealth, health, etc., are all the same. They all abide by the same laws; it's just that business took it upon itself to change all that. They said, 'It's nothing personal, it's just business.' Wrong, it's not just business. Energetically, it is so much more.

We are here on this planet for two reasons.

1. To learn, grow and evolve.
2. To serve.

When that is the approach of a business, when everyone is in it together to learn, grow and evolve and the philosophy is purely to serve, then it is never about the money. Business flipped that and made it all about the money. 'Money, Money, Money ... in a rich man's world,' as ABBA sang.

If the focus is just on money, forget it. Money is purely a by-product of service. If you care about the person more than you care about the money, you will make more money by the simple universal law of reciprocity.

I've heard a lot about workplace culture and in most places, it sucks because ultimately the wrong people with the wrong energy and intentions are in the wrong roles. It is not a mutual recipe for success.

It's all about performance, KPIs and carrot dangling. What can we get out of you to perform? What incentives are just out of your reach that we can pop into your psyche so you give us more? Don't get me wrong. I have had some great targets and some great rewards for hitting them, however once I achieved them, I crashed each time. The reason was that I was filling up from the outside instead of fuelling myself from the inside. I always got my greatest results when the reason I was showing up had meaning. If I genuinely believed in what I was doing for the greater good, I excelled. When I did not, I lost motivation and the drive to give myself to it fully.

When companies work with their individuals to understand why they are in the business and what they want to achieve from it, they can then turn it into a collaborative exercise that mutually benefits the company, the 'business partners' and the customers. When companies look for win-win, they are good. When they look for win-win-win, they are the greatest.

That's truly when everyone's in it together.

Chapter 8

CREATING CONNECTION

'Rapport is the ultimate tool for producing results with other people. No matter what you want in your life, if you can develop rapport with the right people, you'll be able to fill their needs, and they will be able to fill yours.'

TONY ROBBINS

Successful sales leaders master very quickly the art of establishing rapport and building trust.

Interestingly, you never really get a second chance. You only have a limited amount of time to gain people's subconscious trust before they have deliberated internally on their judgement. Not what you do, what you sell or how you do it. Make no mistake, it is you as a person they are judging initially!

That was the reason I learned NLP. Not to be a master manipulator, but to learn the subtle art of subconscious rapport.

Subconscious rapport is about perfecting only three things:

1. Physicality — the body language we use.
2. Tonality — how we say things.
3. Word tracks — the actual words we use.

Physicality is 55% of all communication, tonality is 38% and the words we use make up only 7% of all human interaction.

I find it fascinating that word tracks are only 7% of the entire equation, considering how many salespeople think they will get more deals by talking the ears off their prospects. Wrong! Especially considering that the average person speaks between 10,000 and 20,000 words a day! Knowing the statistics about communication above, have you ever thought about how you communicate with others? It really is fascinating once you learn and observe it.

PHYSICALITY

So, let's break this down a bit. Firstly, what is rapport? According to mindtools.com:

> 'Rapport forms the basis of meaningful, close and harmonious relationships between people. It's the sense of connection that you get when you meet someone you like and trust, and whose point of view you understand. It's the bond that forms when you discover that you share one another's values and priorities in life.'

Hmm ... I do not see the word 'selling' in this statement.

When we are in synchronicity with somebody, the transaction happens naturally, organically. In fact, it is not a sale, it is a solution.

Let's now look at what you need to do to create perfect rapport with anyone.

You will remember I mentioned earlier that people don't care how much you know until they know how much you care, right? Does that mean you must become their best friend? No. It simply means taking an interest in the other person and more so, just listening to what they have to say.

We as humans are social creatures. We like being in the company of other people. It is part of our genetic makeup, which is why 55% of all transactions are physical. Now, you might say that's great if your role is face to face, but what if my sales role is telephone based? Well, we will get to that when we discuss tonality and word tracks.

Firstly, we are energetic beings. We have a thing called a gut feeling and intuition. And our gut feeling is never wrong. (Can you recall following your intuition and it being wrong? Compared to following your head and getting it wrong?)

Let me give you an example.

Have you ever walked into a room and felt the energy of someone in a corner and thought, *'Oh, I don't like that'*? Or somebody has come up to you and you felt extremely uncomfortable?

Of course you have! We all have. So, knowing this, imagine yourself walking into a room and somebody having that instant feeling towards you? How are you ever going to do business with that person if they instantly have a negative feeling towards you? No doubt they will take a lot of convincing and in most cases, it won't work, because you must convince them!

As Dale Carnegie says, *'Those convinced against their will are of the same opinion still.'*

So how do you overcome this and how do you naturally make people trust you?

It's simple: by not overpowering them with your bullshit!

Start by how you dress and look. I touched a little on this before, but I personally feel that nobody likes seeing somebody polished, schmick and out there making a statement. Everybody knows it is bravado. Big fashion statements scream of low self-esteem. Slick hair-dos, the overpowering smell of half a bottle of cologne, the sleek, trendy power suits and the flamboyant shoes ... Ahh, the typical salesperson.

Is that how you want to be seen? I do not, but I do love looking and feeling good.

You want to take pride in how you look and feel. I am more impressed by authentic people being their natural selves and expressing self-confidence from the inside, not creating an image of what they want others to believe them to be on the outside. There is a massive difference between leadership selling and schmick selling. You can look great, or you can go over the top. Work it out.

The next step is to mirror your potential client by mimicking their gestures. BUT ... do it subtly. If you mirror them 100%, they'll know you are mocking them. When mirroring somebody's behaviour, it needs to feel similar to their own, but not exactly the same.

For example, if they are standing with their left foot crossed over their right foot, you will want to take a similar stance. If they lean to one side, mirror that. If their arms are crossed or they have a hand in their pocket, do a similar gesture. Just ensure your moves are slow and subtle, otherwise you will come across as mocking them, and then it's game over! When you are in true rapport, this automatically happens naturally.

You must also be sincere. People can smell insincerity a mile away. Genuine leaders who are authentic always come across with sincerity and honest empathy.

When introducing yourself, reach out for their hand and quickly gauge how they shake hands. Let them lead. Many times, I have had people come to me and squeeze my hand. This is so overpowering and in many cases, a sign of domination. You never want to dominate; that is what managers and dictators do.

Sales animals who thrive on closing want to dominate their prey all the time. It makes me sick to think they can bully someone into buying.

Quickly understand their handshake, then give yours with slightly less pressure than theirs. They will feel comfortable and ready to talk at that point.

TONALITY

Now, let's discuss tonality, the 38% of communication.

Every person has a different toned voice. Some are high pitched, some low pitched, some people speak really fast, others speak really slowly, some draw out their speech, others are short and sharp, and so on.

It's like going for singing lessons and the teacher gets you to explore the range of your vocals.

When it comes to building rapport, tonality is incredibly important, especially if you have a telephone-based role.

I spent a good 15 years selling over the phones and always earned a high six figures from doing so.

When working on the phones, you miss out entirely on the physicality of the sale because obviously you are not in the same room and you cannot see the other person.

The 55% of communication is now gone and the last 45% becomes everything!

The key to great phone-based salespeople who do exceptionally well is their natural leadership.

Tonality uses the same principle as physically matching the other person's body language, only with the tone of voice.

Listening skills are imperative when it comes to tonality. Have you ever wondered why we were born with two ears and one mouth? Simple. Listen more, speak less!

You want to understand, clearly and quickly, exactly how the other person communicates. Once you have got it, mirror them subtly. This naturally puts them at ease and they begin to trust you. Then you can slowly back off and be yourself again to enjoy a free-flowing natural conversation.

Please understand there is a massive difference between naturally mirroring a person's communication style and mimicking or imitating them. If you're unable to, even though it creates rapport very quickly, then I suggest you don't do it.

The reason it works so well is that everybody loves the sound of their own voice. When you sound familiar to them, they trust you more and this opens the doors to more natural and authentic conversations. As the leader of the conversation, you can ask questions that get them to share much more information.

It is like the example I gave earlier of distancing yourself when you do not like the feel or energy of someone in a room. On the other hand, if you are comfortable, you will begin to open up.

If you mirror someone for the wrong reasons and with the wrong intentions, you will be found out and this will ultimately affect your credibility and that of the organisation you are representing. Selling through leadership is again about being of service and simply providing a solution to problems. These little tools unlock the crossed arms a bit quicker and allow you in with less fuss.

WORD TRACKS

Lastly, we look at the final 7%, our word tracks.

Understanding words only makes up 7% of our communication, so how do we maximise that through our leadership?

A sales leader listens carefully to what people say and how they say it.

Every person has a unique way about speaking with the word track they use. Pay close attention to their word tracks. If they say the word 'mate', you say the word 'mate'. If they say, 'the dollars' instead of 'money', you say the same. See what I'm saying? Just make sure you use it in the same context, so it doesn't sound weird.

OPEN-ENDED QUESTIONS

Finally, the best thing to do when communicating is to lead with open-ended questions. These start with 'what', 'why', 'when', 'how' and so on, and allow you to establish a longer conversation, which builds more trust and enables you to understand each other more.

Leading with closed-ended questions will get you nowhere. Closed-ended questions, such as 'do you' or 'are you', etc., lead to one-word answers.

I heard years ago about the sales strategy of getting people to say 'yes' multiple times in a presentation. Then, when it is time for the closing questions, the presenter continues with more questions requiring 'yes' answers. That is manipulation 101; it is selling through mind control, not with integrity through leadership. When people do this to me, I tune right out. They lose me straightaway because I know what they are doing and why they are doing it. I know it is purely for the sale and not with my best interests at heart.

Another thing to remember is that less is more. Conserve your words, conserve your energy and only say what needs to be said. We tend to over-complicate things and I learned many years ago that if it is not necessary to say, it is necessary NOT to say it.

This really is all about being totally present and genuine in your communication.

Chapter 9

STOP CHEWING MY EARS OFF

'People do not buy goods and services. They buy relationships, stories and magic.'

SETH GODIN

Did you know that human beings think in pictures and learn through stories? It's the metaphors in those stories that we get our learnings from. Every movie you see or song you have sung are all stories, with hidden or open messages. It is through these stories we get the chance to visualise ourselves in certain roles and situations. We get to learn from others and what they have done through the story they share. However, be aware not to let the truth get in the way of a good story.

I've seen salespeople make up unbelievable stories to convince people to buy their products. And I have also seen a good story help me decide what I wanted to do.

> We have a 15-year-old Japanese Spitz dog, Sumo, who had bad teeth. We agonised for months over what to do because of his age. Our vet could not tell us what to do. We were dealing with an old dog. A general anaesthetic is required for all dental work and because of his age, there was a high chance that he would not wake up after it. We were also dealing with his quality of life because his teeth were so bad, and we could tell how sore he was based on his behaviour.
>
> Matt, our vet, gave us many different examples of success and failure stories to consider when making our decision about what was right for Sumo and us. Ultimately, we decided to go ahead with the risk and have the procedure done. Luckily, it was the best decision — even though in life and death matters, hindsight is a wonderful thing.
>
> The stories Matt shared helped us make our decision. For him, this was a sale — he made money from our decision — but his intentions were not to get the sale, or to make money, they were all about what was best for our dog.

This is the opposite from a salesperson who just doesn't shut up! Some want to explain everything single thing to you, which is irrelevant in the sales process. It drives me crazy because more often than not, these salespeople actually lose the deal and have no idea why.

Our vet didn't mention the details of the procedure. Our decision was based purely on the result. That said, I do appreciate in business that there are times when it is vital to know the details.

FOUR TYPES OF PURCHASERS

From my experience in all types of selling, there really are only four types of purchasers.

THEY KNOW WHAT THEY WANT

This type of purchaser is simple to assist. An old sales manager of mine once told me, 'If a man wants a green wooden horse with only one leg, that's what you sell them.' In some cases, it is fair that if somebody knows what they want, our job as salespeople is to be of service and supply. They may already have done their research, or they know they are looking for something specific to fill a void. It is the simplest of sales to make, so why try and screw it up?

Do you remember me saying, 'a man convinced against his will is of the same opinion still'? If you follow that principle, then this type of customer will always feel great because you have provided them with exactly what they wanted. Period. The common acronym 'KISS' — **Keep It Simple Stupid** — makes complete sense.

I don't understand why some salespeople feel the need to over-complicate things.

In my career I have trained hundreds of salespeople in different companies, across multiple industries, each having a proven method, along with scripts and processes and procedures to follow. Yet many salespeople went off and did their own thing. Mind-blowingly stupid!

If you simply listen to what the customer wants and provide them with exactly that, they will never experience buyer's remorse or have a genuine reason to return the product. As the salesperson, your job is simply to be the solution provider and facilitate the transaction with ease.

It really irritates me when I see people wanting to purchase something but who then get sold into something else because the salesperson thinks it is better, or worse still, because the company wants to get rid of it. How is that better for the customer? Have you ever experienced this yourself?

> It reminds me of a time when I went to my local doctors because I had sinus problems. I have had sinus problems for many years and finally I decided to get a referral to an ear, nose and throat specialist to see what was going on. These were specific needs, and I knew exactly what I wanted, but the doctor had different ideas.
>
> He looked at me and asked how old I was, how many drinks I had each day or week, what my diet was like, how often I exercised. He took my blood pressure and asked if any members of my family had ever had cancer. The standard questions and checks.
>
> I replied yes, and before I knew it, he had picked up his mobile phone — yes, his mobile phone — called a doctor specialist friend of his and talked in his native tongue in front of me, then wrote me a referral to have my prostate checked. WTF was that? Were kickbacks involved and he did really have my best interests at heart?

> This blew me away. I went in for my nose and walked out for my bum! I could not believe it. The referral went straight into the bin and I have never been back since.

Now you may be asking why I am bringing this up in a sales book? Because doctors are salespeople too! As soon as you accept their diagnosis, especially when it involves drugs and procedures, you have been sold to. In many cases, they may also instil in you new beliefs that may or may not be true.

CUSTOMERS WHO THINK THEY KNOW WHAT THEY WANT

Next is the customer who thinks they know what they want. They have a basic idea and are looking for a little guidance to ensure they are making the right decision. Yes, you must provide them with some specific info if required, but people do generally get lost in the specifics. The more information provided, the lower the chance of a decision, because of confusion. The mind can only process so much information before it overloads and shuts down. You will know this yourself. Have you ever found yourself zoning out? As soon as you hit that point, your brain simply cannot process any more information.

Because we think in pictures (think back to my examples of the real estate agents painting two great pictures to sell their houses), most people cannot decide on specifics, unless you are an analytical person and that is how you are wired to think. Talking that language to an IT geek or an engineer is great, but talk that way to an artist or a farmer and the sale is lost.

Generally, when you give people a little information, they will ask questions and you can then easily add plenty of examples. It is the story they perceive in their imagination that will help them come to the decision to buy.

I am often asked, how do I get other people to visualise what I am saying? That is the simplest part. All you have to do is ask them to 'imagine' and you then tell them a story. They will see it clearly. You can give many examples and scenarios to help them make the right decision — for them.

CUSTOMERS WHO HAVE LITTLE IDEA WHAT THEY WANT

These types of customers only have a basic idea of what they want. As I mentioned earlier, telling is not selling. So, let's put it in context.

Say a family needs a new car. How many variations of car options are there? So many! Other than knowing they need a new car, it is time to start discovering more about the family — their needs, desires and wants.

This is all done by asking open-ended questions and having great listening skills. We have all heard about the dodgy car salesman selling lemons to people that just did not suit them. Such stories are told by those who have been 'sold' into buying something by a fast-talking opportunistic salesperson.

A great sales leader will take the time to truly understand the client's needs and help them understand what they actually want. They ask open-ended questions so that it becomes a process of elimination. Such questions may include, 'How many people are in your family?' 'What pets do you have?' 'What do you want the vehicle for — to tow a trailer or a caravan or a jetski?' 'What is important to you in a car?' 'Are you looking for specific features or colours?' 'What is your preference — sedan, SUV or wagon?' 'How much driving do you do each year?'

Now a disclaimer. I have never sold a car before, but I know I'd be great at it because it really is that simple. Once you have rapport, you can keep asking questions and your prospective client will be willing to answer. If you are sleezy, abrupt, forceful or non-authentic, forget it. The potential client will be turned right off, and the sales opportunity will be lost. You need to be a problem solver working out a solution with them that is suitable to their needs.

It becomes a rewarding exchange because you are being of service and helping someone, genuinely. The focus is 100% on the customer, not your pay cheque.

CUSTOMERS WHO HAVE NO IDEA WHAT THEY WANT

These people are often sold to when they are not even looking to buy. Taking advantage of these consumers really ticks me off and it is the type of sales I'd like to eradicate from the world. This is the ocean most direct sales companies go fishing in.

People who do not know what they want are still very much in research mode. It is a lot harder to get an immediate answer, which is what many salespeople are looking for. When I was dealing with this type of customer, the strategy that worked best for me was to forget about the sale 'today', and work on the 'see me, believe me, trust me' model of building a relationship. You then give yourself the highest possible chance for success later.

When you do a good job of that, they will remember you and want to come back and they'll personally ask for you. That's what I do — ensure that the salesperson who treated me right gets the figures and commission for their efforts.

Taking this one step further, as I mentioned earlier, people do not remember what you told them, they only remember how you made them feel. If you are detached, honest and obliging, why would they want to deal with anyone else? You will be your own best marketing. Your clients become screaming fans of you, not what you do or what you sell, and they'll be your greatest referral source by telling all their friends how great you are.

See me, believe me, TRUST me … When you have created trust, these people you do not know will want to do business with you, simply because they too want to feel the same afterwards.

Tell me, would you rather build your business and sales career that way, through word of mouth and referral, or through cold calling 100 people per day? Working smarter not harder was always my philosophy, and so much better for your mindset and attitude. Jim Rohn always said work harder on yourself than you do on your business. So that is what I did!

Going back to the people who do not know what they want, we need to leave them with a picture in their mind of what they want. An important thing to know is that after each day passes, the retention of whatever information you have shared with them is lost — approximately 20% per day, so after five days, everything you shared is out the window.

It pays to be on the front foot. A true leader will always get a name, number and email address to follow up. My rule of thumb is two to three follow-ups only, and it's always best to make the second follow-up 48 hours after the first. It is important to remain detached from the outcome. Forty-eight hours does not show any level of desperateness.

Then I would call again the following day. If there is no response, I would give it another 48 to 72 hours. Each call will remind them that you are there, and you care about them. If they are serious buyers, they will always come back to you.

One massive point of difference I've found between my approach and that of other salespeople is that on my last call, I let them know that it will be my final call. Doing so tells them you are not desperate for the business, your time is important and must be valued and you will not be hassling them. Nobody likes being forced into something. The truth is, if we want something, we do not need to be hassled to buy it. We do it naturally.

It embarrasses me to say that I have been in direct sales for a long time and I've seen salespeople use all the tricks in the book to get an instant, unwanted sale on a product that will never be used. Unfortunately, if you want to earn great money in sales, you must be able to close deals all the time, despite the cost. Most companies that employ direct salespeople and ask them to create sales, don't have a product people want or need. I have worked in several shady industries — or so I found out later. When I first started, they sold me on how wonderful they were and what a difference they made, only to find out three or six months later they were all full of shit.

If I had my time again I'm not sure I would do anything differently because I know, with the skills I have, when aligned with the right company that truly makes a difference to people's lives, I will always be remembered as the person who helped change lives for the better.

Chapter 10

I AM NOT AFRAID OF YOU

'Success is not final, failure is not fatal, it's the courage to continue that matters.'

WINSTON CHURCHILL

Fear is the biggest killer of any potential salesperson and the number one reason most people quit many things in life or work.

Wikipedia describes fear as: 'Fear is an **emotion induced by perceived danger or threat**, which causes physiological changes and ultimately behavioural changes, such as fleeing, hiding, or freezing from perceived traumatic events. Fear in human beings may occur in response to a certain stimulus occurring in the present, or in anticipation or expectation of a future threat perceived as a risk to oneself. The fear response arises from the perception of danger leading to confrontation with or escape from/avoiding the threat (also known as the fight-or-flight response), which in extreme cases of fear (horror and terror) can be a freeze response or paralysis.'

And rejection:

'In psychology, an interpersonal situation that occurs when a person or group of people exclude an individual from a social relationship.'

FEAR

If you ask any salesperson why they weren't successful, you'll find it's usually because of fear, or the fear of rejection.

It's understandable that people are afraid of being harmed, or being in danger or even being excluded from things, but WTF does that have to do with picking up a telephone, or walking into an office to engage in building business or achieving a sales result?

Let me break it down for you.

F.E.A.R. stands for False, Evidence, Appearing, Real.

While fear is a perfectly natural emotion for people, I learned after years of personal development that ultimately, deep down, people are only afraid of two things.

1. The feeling of not being enough.
2. Not being loved or accepted if we're not enough.

When I was managing a telesales call centre, I used to observe the sales people staring at the phones instead of picking them up and dialling.

Is cold calling a hard thing to do? Nope, you just pick up the phone, dial the number and speak to somebody who answers. Simple, right? Wrong!

For most, this was the toughest gig of their lives. Yet, if they said to the other person on the line, 'Sorry wrong number,' they would find that the answer was almost always, 'All good, no problem.'

However, most people would rather take the easier route by quitting and leaving the job, instead of working through the fear and mastering it.

I asked the people I was coaching, 'What are you afraid of? The phone is only plastic, it cannot physically harm you.' Yet in many cases, they were paralysed by it.

If you refer back to what I wrote about human connection, 38% of rapport building is tonality and 7% of communication is words. So the 45% of human interaction via the phone blew people away. Because you cannot even see the other person, it proves it's all made up in your head!

It's a different story for those who cold call face to face, because they can psych themselves up and just walk into the room.

Moving from cold calling to warm or hot leads, where people are calling in to speak to you or are actively looking for your service and requesting information, if you display fear it will cost you a sale every time.

With the fear of not being enough, self-worth raises its ugly head again!

Society has drummed into people that they are not worth it. That is why people accept low-paying jobs and conditions and do little about it. In many ways it is a form of slavery.

Leaders do not have this attitude at all. They know what they are worth, and so their attitude to sales is vastly different.

When I started my journey in sales, I knew I needed to improve and understand myself more, which was why I went down the path of personal development. During this time, I was introduced to the term 'CANI'. CANI stands for Constant And Never-ending IMPROVEMENT in Kaizen philosophy.

As a leader, the stronger your leadership skills become, the better your sales results naturally grow. This is because as a rule, people like to be led.

If your self-worth and self-belief are low, forget sales. It simply isn't for you. And yet in saying that, what career would be? Everything in life revolves around interacting with people and supporting one another. A great way of becoming a better leader is to commit to your personal growth and evolution. Read one book a month and make personal development part of your continual growth mindset. Nowadays, we have Audible, Spotify and iTunes where we can listen to books, podcasts and series wherever we are. Immerse yourself in it and become the leader you were born to be!

Taking rejection personally is a huge obstacle to overcome. It really is. You simply need to be resilient in sales. A great salesperson does not let this stuff affect their emotional state. They understand it is part of the game.

I remember smashing the phones to make sales, making call after call, day after day. It can get demoralising when you get nowhere and every call is a 'no'. Prospecting, prospecting, prospecting … It's like that because of the daily hounding of people to buy shit. You become just another salesperson approaching another potential unsuspecting buyer.

It then becomes about making the call rather than why you are making the call. The focus is in the wrong place.

In sales that result directly from marketing, it's a bit different as people are responding to advertising or coming to you for a reason. Rest assured, you can do everything right and still not get the sale. Understand that people are not saying 'no' to you as a person, they are saying 'no' to the opportunity you present.

My tip in this case is to surround yourself with an energetic shield every day. Imagine a blue bubble around yourself which is protecting you, which in turn protects your mindset and makes you like Teflon. Don't let the crap stick, don't take it personally, understand the intention behind WHY you are prospecting, and you'll find life will be so much better!

I also suggest keeping yourself grounded. If you have your energy in check, you will approach all matters very differently. The easiest way to keep yourself grounded is to take your shoes off and stand on the earth. It must be earth, or sand, dirt, grass, rocks, etc. Definitely not concrete. Do this every day for 15 minutes and your entire physiology will change.

LOVE AND ACCEPTANCE

Now, let's look at the second point of being loved and accepted.

Our number one human need is to be loved. First, however, we need to love and like ourselves. I mean, how can others love and like us if we do not love or like ourselves? Look at babies; that is all they need to survive. Giving the right foundation in life is everything and if your foundation is a little skewiff, then that's even more reason to work on yourself.

You are your greatest investment in life — period.

Everybody wants to be valued. Everybody wants to be accepted. Everybody wants to be loved. The universal law is reciprocity — give first to receive next.

Yet in sales and business, where is the love, where is the acceptance, the appreciation or the gratitude? There is none. It is cold and emotionless, the complete opposite of what it means to be human. How did it ever get this way?

In sales, a leader's intentions are to serve. A closer's intentions are to take.

FEAR OF FAILURE

Similar to the fear of rejection is the fear of failure. People who are afraid of failure are simply afraid of the perceived judgement of others, not of the act itself.

According to Wikipedia, failure is 'the state or condition of not meeting a desirable or intended objective and may be viewed as the opposite of success'.

Hmm, let's dissect that. And what if I flip it on its head? If success is 'the achievement of a desired result', how does one succeed at something? Does everyone always succeed at the first attempt?

Michael Jordan: *'I've missed more than 9000 shots in my career.'*

Tiger Woods: *'The greatest thing about tomorrow, is I will be better than I am today.'*

Roger Federer: *'You have to put in a lot of sacrifice and effort for sometimes little reward but you have to know that if you put in the right effort the reward will come.'*

Sylvester Stallone: *'Success is usually the culmination of controlling failures. Going on one more round, when you don't think you can, that's what makes all the difference in your life.'*

Do you see the messages here? Success is the sum of constant, repeated failures over a long time, until you get the desired result.

As Winston Churchill said:

'Success is stumbling from failure to failure with no loss of enthusiasm.'

Do you recall me stating it takes 10,000 hours to become an expert at something? So, the difference between somebody who does succeed, versus somebody who does not, is the repeated hours of failure.

Rejection is simply part of that learning. Each failure is feedback on what to do differently next time.

I mentioned earlier, there is a great book called *Go For No! Yes Is the Destination, No Is How You Get There* by Andrea Waltz and Richard Fenton. Read it and start realising that no matter what happens, your life is never in danger when you are prospecting. No physical harm can come to you. So be the infant, expect you have a learning curve to go through and live outside of your comfort zone until you acquire the skills to be a master salesperson.

The next step in overcoming the fear of rejection or failure is learning the art of detachment.

'If you want to make everyone happy, don't be a leader, sell ice cream.'

STEVE JOBS

That is a fascinating statement from an incredible man who changed the world. His vision, his goals, his dedication, his never-give-in attitude, his commitment, his determination and his courage are what made the difference.

Like I used to tell all my salespeople, 'Fail your way to success.' True learning comes from repeated trial and error.

Chapter 11

THE PLAN OF ATTACK

'Success is the sum of small efforts, repeated day in and day out.'

ROBERT COLLIER

One of the things I notice about successful salespeople is that they are extremely well organised, and they know how to maximise their time. It is not about how many hours you work; it is about making the most of the time and opportunities you have while being the best version of yourself in those hours.

Time is a precious commodity. It is the only thing in life we never get back. An assertive sales leader knows exactly what they need to do and they simply get on with it.

I learned many years ago, if you need something done, give it to the busiest person around. Any ideas why? Well, the busiest people are action takers and they get shit done! They don't have time for excuses, and they honour their commitments.

I'm not talking here about people who say, 'I'm too busy.' Saying they are busy is not the reason they cannot do it, it is just an excuse from a mediocre person who does not see it as a priority.

A great salesperson will always 'make' the time because they understand the benefits of, and the reasons for doing their best. That is why they are natural leaders. Throughout my career, my bosses always asked me to do more for them, and I often wondered why. It was not because they expected me to do more than the others, it was because they knew it would always get done.

In years to come, I found the more strategic I became with my time, the more time I had to do extra activities. I also found that because I was truly busy, I became less attached to the outcome and more inclined to keep following through. I was on purpose, and it helped me learn how to prioritise tasks.

One key factor is not to get caught up in the busyness of it, and to remain focused on the task at hand. Many people in sales are what I call 'I'm gonna' people: 'I'm gonna get to that soon.' 'I was going to do that next …' 'I was going to call you back but you beat me to it.' 'I was going to …'

I think you get the point.

There is no place for people who behave like that in sales. Personally, I cannot stand it. It's incredibly unprofessional and often disrespectful. These types of salespeople usually find themselves working for minimum wages, and I guarantee they are the ones who always complain and whine about how hard it is, that it's not fair, why someone else got the promotion or pay rise … Ultimately, they always get caught out and are found wanting.

We all have the same amount of time per day to get our desired results. Twenty-four hours. Those who get more out of their days are simply strategic with their time.

I find the easiest way is to map out my day in an electronic dairy. When setting it up, it's important to separate personal, family and work time. It also helps to colour code it.

Most people forget to look after themselves first. They are so busy with work, family, pets, kids, sports etc. that life becomes all-consuming. Welcome to the 'Rat Race'. At one time, I found myself caught in the trap of doing things for everyone else. My work became all about the commitments I needed to maintain for the greater good of my family, and I lost focus on ensuring my life was fulfilling.

When I was so determined to succeed, my work became my life. It became more important than my wife, my kids, my health and myself. I subscribed to the bullshit notion of 'how "badly" do you want it?' Or, 'what are you prepared to "sacrifice" to get it'. Seems I was sacrificing myself.

That was when I was at my heaviest and most unhealthy. That was when I lost contact with many friends and family because I was always busy doing other things. That was when I felt early signs of depression setting in. It was also when regret began to creep in because I felt I was losing out on life for 'work success'.

I remember reading an article by Susie Steiner in *The Guardian* in 2012 about the top five regrets a palliative care nurse heard from dying people. The number one regret was 'I wish I hadn't worked so hard.' And that got me thinking about how I was showing up in my life and what I wanted instead.

In my first business I learned about the 'daily method of operation' (DMO), it made all the difference. (DMO is a popular phrase in the USA but not so much in Australia.) Finally, I could make sense of it all and systemise it to my advantage.

Having a happy and well-balanced life leads to much better performance at work. We need to consider that our work is an extension of us, simply a part of our life, not our life itself. I found that by doing more in areas of my life that filled me up on the inside helped my outside world blossom accordingly.

THE STRATEGY

So let's map it all out for you.

COLOUR CODING

First, work out everything you want and need to do each day or week and then make it visual by assigning colours to it. Being visual gives it more meaning and feeling.

You can use any colours that resonate with you personally. This is what I do:

Personal activity time	Blue
Family activity time (kids)	Yellow
Work activity time	Green
Partner activity time	Red
Relationships/catch-ups	Purple

I chose blue for my personal activities because it is my favourite colour. Also, it is the colour of the sky and the sea, and it induces calm and conveys serenity. When I see lots of blue in my diary, I know I am doing stuff that is for me and that makes me happier and more at peace. It also shows me every day what I get to do for myself, and that brings me joy. I have a lot of gratitude for this because by design, I am living the life I want.

Yellow is for my kids' activities because it is uplifting. It's also the colour of sunshine, which is a youthful and fresh energy, like my kids. My father was not available for me growing up. He was too busy working. When I had kids, I made a conscious decision that they were my life, and I wanted to enjoy every minute of it, so having rays of sunshine fills me right up.

I chose red for my wife, as it's the combination of the passion and love I have for her. When I see the red in my diary, it fills my heart with more of the great stuff.

Green is for my work activities because it is the colour of nature. It encourages growth and good health, two important things when it comes to my work. Also, green is symbolically associated with money (the greenback), so for me it encompasses total abundance. That makes me happy too!

Purple is the colour I use for connection. I love creating deep and meaningful friendships with people. With our friends and family, we talk openly about anything and everything. Friends to us are an especially important part of our spiritual soul journey and we love nourishing it regularly by spending quality time with people we love. Purple is perfect for that!

You can see how when there is meaning in our lives, we get to live more authentically and with integrity.

So, now you have that all sorted out, it's time to map out your week!

MAPPING OUT A WORK WEEK EXAMPLE

Start with yourself. Put everything personal in your diary first: gym, sport, exercise, art, music, personal development, meditation … Anything at all that is your special time.

This is what my weekly diary might look like.

5–6 am (Blue)	Exercise, Listen to PD in car to and from gym, meditate
6–7 am (Green)	Work
7–9 am (Yellow)	Get breakfast, take kids to school
9 am–2.45 pm (Green)	Work
2.45–3.30 pm (Yellow)	School pick-up
3.30 pm–6 pm (Green/Yellow)	Work/After-school Activities
6–7.30 pm (Purple)	Dinner with Family/Friends
7.30–9.30pm (Red)	Time with my wife

MAPPING OUT A WEEKEND EXAMPLE

6–7 am (Blue)	Exercise, listen to PD, meditate
8–11 am (Yellow)	Kids' activities
11 am–12 pm (Green)	Shopping
12–8 pm (Purple)	Time with friends/family
8–9 pm (Red)	Time with my wife

If we have after-school activities for the kids, they are included and colour coded. Best part is I can still do work stuff in between my family's commitments. For example, if I am waiting for my kids at after-school activities, I can multitask, so I generally schedule follow-up calls or respond to emails while watching my kids!

I coach my son's football and cricket teams, so during training, that's all marked blue because it's something that's for me. I take him and my daughters to football practice, music, drama, karate, singing etc and they are all marked yellow.

My calendar is synched with my wife's. When she does something of her own, she adds it to my calendar in light blue. That way, I know her movements and can work around that when need be, and she can see all my commitments too.

Seeing it all mapped out in front of you, you know exactly what time is dedicated to what and there is no messing about.

Life should be a healthy balance of work, rest and play.

Chapter 12

THE GAME!

'Focus on being productive instead of busy.'

TIM FERRISS

THE GAME PART 1
PROSPECTING

Prospecting is the lifeline of every salesperson's success and ultimately every business' success. It is the one thing that is a constant, yet it is also the one thing that most salespeople fail at.

Prospecting is the first step in the **sales** process, identifying potential customers, aka prospects. The goal of **prospecting** is to develop a database of likely customers and then systematically communicate with them in the hopes of converting them from potential customer to current customer.

An important caveat when you are prospecting is to avoid pre-judging a potential customer — deciding that they won't buy from you for no other reason than that you have judged them as a non-prospect. It just might be that the very person you think isn't going to buy is the one who does — or would have, if you hadn't dismissed them as a prospect.

Different types of prospecting include:

- cold calling
- warm calling
- responding to incoming enquiries from brand marketing and direct marketing campaigns via print and online media/social media
- Google searches
- referrals.

Whatever the means by which the lead or customers come, it's all about building a connection and a relationship for a future purchase.

As a sales representative, I was initially responsible for door knocking to introduce myself and our services. It did not stop there.

Doing a one-off introduction would not have got me anywhere. People would forget me as soon as I'd left.

Once you've broken the ice, constant communication and repeat connection is important in order to be at the forefront of people's minds.

> That's why the big companies spend millions of dollars each year on marketing — to keep them at the forefront of your mind. Look at Coke, McDonald's, Nike, large electrical retailers, etc. In their advertising campaigns,

they are brainwashing you subconsciously, in the hope that one day when you need their product, you will go to them and not their competitors.

Did you know that back in the 80s, Coca-Cola used to advertise subliminal messages during movies? Yep, for a millisecond they would throw in a picture of Coke right in the middle of the movie. It was so fast that consciously, movie-goers would not pick it up, yet all of a sudden they'd be thirsty and want to buy a Coke!

Brainwashing 101... Crazy, hey?

Most reps have a designated territory or client base to cover. Their number one role is to sell something today, as instructed by the business owners and managers, but 'repping' is much more than that. It is account management from the initial introduction onwards. You need to be a people person who can be the eventual solution to what the client needs.

Remember, it is about 'see me, believe me and then trust me', building rapport — 55% of what we do is physical, so making a good impression while prospecting is important. Be genuine with it and you will go far. If you go straight in for the kill, you will be killed off first. People smell insincerity a mile away.

KEEP SHOWING UP

Once you have their trust, people will test you out and buy once. If you do a good job and deliver on what you promise, they will buy again. A great salesperson is one who gets repeat business, and that repeat business turns into a flow of ongoing referral business.

It is never about the cost of the product. It is always about delivering on your promise, the service you provide and the rapport you have built. People buy off people.

A great face-to-face salesperson is one who has incredible self-confidence, a warm, genuine approach and a pleasant attitude. They want to be of service. Why most salespeople fail at prospecting is the fear of meeting and socialising with people and the lack of drive to keep going. Face-to-face rejection is the toughest of all to work through because there is no hiding. It is right there in your face.

You need to use emotional regulation and not take it personally. As a representative, you are trying to win over the customer. They may already have a supplier for the product or service you are offering, so why would they want to buy from you instead? Initially, they probably won't. However, when you continually show up and build a relationship with the customer, you will find that a time will come when they can't get what they want from their preferred supplier and need to find it elsewhere. That will be you.

'Keep showing up' is something that most salespeople fail to do when prospecting. The only reason I was successful in face-to-face selling was because I kept showing up. In fact, the reason I've been successful in everything I've done is because I keep showing up, despite setbacks.

BE ACCOUNTABLE

After I unintentionally lost my first business, I decided to embark on accountability coaching. I am a particularly good coach and mentor and people who followed my lead always got incredible results. Many of clients were in sales and wanting to make more money. It was easy to see their financial blockages from where I sat. It was also easy to understand their accountability issues. What was even more fascinating was the number of people who struggled signing their accountability contract with me.

The contract was not about locking them in to my program, it was about holding them accountable to a higher level and ensuring they would commit to themselves and their goals. It also gave me permission to ask the hard questions necessary in order to ensure they stayed on the path.

After all my years in sales and business, I found this was the major difference between success and failure. Accountability is having courage to keep showing up. Committing to yourself. However, left to their own devices, most people do not have the discipline to see things through. When the going gets tough, the tough get going and the weak disappear. As soon as the weak give themselves an out, they always take it and then generally blame somebody else.

So, face-to-face prospecting is not about the sale right now. It is about showing up, being accountable and knocking on as many doors as you can.

Let me give you a visual about continually filling up your pipeline.

Imagine you have a long cardboard tube, the same as what you would buy from a post office. Now scrunch up sheets of paper into small balls that will fit in the tube, then slowly put them in one by one. Keep filling up the tube with more scrunched-up paper until the tube is almost full. Keep adding more paper into the tube until eventually, a piece will fall out the end.

That is your sale! That is the reward for all the effort you have put in at the beginning, for just showing up without expecting much more. Set the intention to be of value and service. Educate your potential customer on yourself, then your service or product. Be authentic, because if you bullshit your way through, you will get caught out and the opportunity will be lost forever.

PHONE-BASED COLD CALLING

When I moved away from face-to-face sales to phone-based sales, prospecting took on a whole new meaning. I had to do cold calling and I really hated it. Who likes making 100 calls a day? However, one of my mentors taught me that if I wanted to succeed at it, I needed to get to love it.

Looking back, I realised it was the constant rejection of cold calling that I hated, not the actual cold calling itself. It is important to get clear about that, so you can move past it and do what you need to do.

I knew my objectives — how much money I wanted to earn each week — and I knew what I needed to do and how many calls I needed to make to achieve it.

Like it or not, sales is prospecting and lead generation. You must be constantly prospecting and meeting people to sell your product or service. I wasn't one of those salespeople who particularly enjoyed making hundreds of calls every day. I learned early on that if I got better at my craft, I would not need to.

I could simply get my desired results by communicating better with the people I spoke to. Whenever I started at a new company, I would ask how much money their top salesperson was earning. I watched that person's method of operation and learned how they did it.

Working on myself more than on my job was the key, which is why I am such a fan of personal development and communication education. Sales is simple. There is a script, a process, but the conversion rates between a good result and an incredible result are very different. One in three was always my strike rate, no matter where or what I was selling. Increase your strike rate, increase the results.

These days I have learned that the best people to work with are those who are referred to you. I would much rather build relationships because these people naturally become my external sales force. Your network equals your net worth. Everybody asks for recommendations and people would much rather deal with somebody referred to them. The trust levels are so much greater. If you are in real estate, how much easier is it to get a listing from somebody referred to you? If I do a great job and leave a great impression with somebody I have served, then I know it will bring me more business time and time again. Such business is free business, or icing on the cake. It's the continual referral model that will feed you forever.

That is when you know you've prospected well. If your intentions are always on the customer, you handle yourself with honour and integrity and display good values, the universe will always have your back and connect you with the right people.

The other important part of prospecting is to make sure you call back and follow up every single lead and enquiry. Would you believe that there are salespeople who don't ever follow up? Unbelievable! If you don't, how are you ever going to help anyone? You cannot help the customer, you can't help your company and you can't help yourself if you don't do this.

If you have nobody to speak to, go out and find someone. Prospecting 101. Always ensure you finalise every interaction that comes your way. Professionalism 101.

If you just take one thing away from this book, remember that you get paid for prospecting and growing.

THE GAME PART 2
OBJECTIONS

'Our greatest weakness lies in giving up. The most certain way to succeed is to try just one more time.'

THOMAS EDISON

In sales, as in most communications, objections are a natural part of the game and we need to work towards overcoming them. Because objections are grossly misunderstood, most salespeople fail to carry the sale through.

Think back to the direct sales model of selling, where people are approached to buy a product or service they are not looking for, do not want or need. Their objections are real. 'Go away, I'm not interested.' Nobody likes being forced to buy something against their will, which is unfortunately what happens in this case.

It reminds me of an innocent girl at a nightclub with her friends just wanting a fun night out. She's happily dancing, having a great time, not looking for anything else, but the sleazy guy pounces all over her, obviously with completely different intentions, hassling to buy her a drink.

Crappy example, sure, but you get the point.

When direct sales are done over the phone, people can easily hang up and move on. Picture yourself as a cold caller. Could you imagine making anywhere from 100 to 300-plus calls a day and being hung up on the same number of times a day? That has happened to me. It's foul, and it doesn't do the ego much good. In fact, it's soul-destroying for those who don't have a thick skin.

People forget that in a genuine sales process, an objection is a buying signal, especially when questions are being asked at the same time. People are asking you for more help to understand if what you are offering is what they are after. They are looking for more clarification.

When inexperienced salespeople are faced with an objection, they treat it as a 'NO' because they do not understand the underlying meaning. When they treat an objection as a NO rather than working through the underlying issue, it becomes the end of the sales attempt. That is why emotional regulation in sales is so important — taking things professionally, not personally. That is vastly different from having the mindset of a closer and just going for the kill.

Over the years, I've observed various responses by salespeople to handling objections. I've seen the bully pit bull terrier approach, where salespeople force themselves onto a prospective customer to overcome their objections. These salespeople do not listen at all to what the customer is saying to them. They steam-roller them into a corner, make them feel uncomfortable and force them to give in and buy. It becomes a battle of wills and the top dog generally wins by force of nature.

Those poor unsuspecting customers. I've seen some throw what they purchased straight into the bin! Tell me, how is that selling with integrity and authenticity? It's not. It's simply the company pushing the salesperson to get more sales, and the salesperson desperately needing a sale to keep their job or to be top dog on the leader board.

What I find more fascinating is the deeper level of the bully approach, called psychology selling. I spoke about this briefly when explaining NLP. This is a clever sales tactic, tricking the customer's subconscious mind to agree. The salesperson just asks 'yes' questions all the way through until they get the desired result. Here's a personal example of both.

> Get a YES at any cost.
>
> My wife needed a new phone cover for her mobile phone. She knew exactly what she wanted before we got to the shop. We first approached the store in our local shopping centre and the shop assistant asked what we were after.
>
> My wife told him she wanted a leather-look flip case that closed over the top of her phone, and had credit card slots inside. He then showed her a plastic case that wasn't flip and had no credit card slots and asked her to buy it. She said that wasn't what she wanted. He searched all the other cases he had and found a hard cover one. Again, not what she asked for. Yet he still asked her to buy it. Now he had received two legitimate 'NO' objections.
>
> He found a third case, more in line with what Amanda was looking for, except the colours were putrid. She said, 'I don't like those colours,' to which he said, 'That's a popular colour, would you like it?' Face slap. Now we were getting irritated because he was just not listening and was not taking no for an answer. He said, 'Would you like the pink one?' Amanda said, 'No, I'm after a darker colour, blue or black.' He showed her a brown and orange.

> That was all he had and regardless of what we wanted, the customers, his objection handling was based on, taking what he had, and then offering us a special price..
>
> Still not taking no as an answer, he proceeded to bail us up and call his other stall. He said, 'They have what you want, go there.' We did, and they didn't. Such a waste of our time and it did not make us feel good. His idea of objection handling was, 'I don't care what you want or say, I will sell you this instead.' Anyone seen my spew bucket?

I will never forget a former sales manager telling me that I would start selling when I received an objection from a customer. I looked at him as if he was an alien. I used to hate making people do something against their will for money. I have a moral objection to it now. When you come from a space of connection and service, you will see that such companies cannot survive long term with that philosophy. They create a poor reputation for themselves and always get caught out.

> Another example of psychology selling was when we realised that our kids were behind in their maths at school, so we made an appointment for a phone call with a company to enquire about extra tutoring.
>
> I do need to throw in a quick disclaimer here. We did not go searching online, we were referred by a friend, so we already had a small level of trust in the company before we spoke with them.
>
> The salesperson was old school. He was polite, well-spoken and trained to make us think we were right all the way through his spiel. Each time he asked us a

question, it could only be a yes answer. Then he agreed with everything we said, and each time highlighted exactly why we needed to buy their product. Because he took us on the beautiful journey about wanting to help our kids, we actually couldn't disagree with him.

He was following a script and when we asked questions that made him deviate from it, he was skilful in returning to it. He calmly answered each question I threw at him and followed up his answer with questions like, 'Is this great for you?' 'Is this what you want?' 'Can you see *your kids* (bringing the emotion back in) benefiting from this?' I knew he was simply flipping our questions back onto us and waiting until we agreed with him. Each time, he was locking away another 'yes'.

I saw right through his strategy but appreciated how he performed. He was not pushy, overpowering or sleezy. Now I did say 'performed'. Why? Because he was not authentic. He was using a sales pitch. He was late making his phone call to us — my number one pet hate! — and disengaged during the call. We could tell he did not want to be there and that his focus was on getting the call over and done with as quickly as possible — being 7.30 pm. He was what I would call a smooth operator. However, he did his job well and got the sale. We wanted tutoring and he demonstrated how his system would work for our kids.

I want to deviate for a moment and touch on sales that offer no place for raising objections. Examples abound in the seminar and mass education industry, and in new online sales campaigns. These start with a general introduction, pointing out people's deficiencies and getting people to think they want more, deserve more and can be so much more, enticing them with life-changing products and services and new careers — how to be an author, a buyer's advocate, an Airbnb specialist, a life coach … How to sell millions on Amazon, how to be a property developer, how to franchise your business … Whatever the buzz words and opportunities happen to be at the time, they go for people's vulnerabilities.

All have low-priced entry-level products: $47, $79, $99, $297 … I'm sure you'll have seen examples of these. They are designed to whet the appetite for more. It's a drip-feed funnel system. People are subconsciously enticed by the low-level spend and good content — often for the price of a few pizzas!

By marketing to millions and getting thousands of small sales, these businesses pay for the marketing.

What happens next? People are left wanting more, and so the next level purchase kicks in, then the next and the next and before long, they have spent $5,000, $10,000, $25,000, $50,000 or $100,000 plus.

This approach to direct sales is now very common and for me, it's a turn-off. I'm waiting for the big-ticket sell. Because of the process, I now choose not to even follow through on many opportunities, despite how good the material may be.

As I said at the beginning of this example: how does this fit into the category of objection handling? It does not, because there is none. It's all about impulse buying.

The direct sales industry knows there is always a new person entering the market who does not yet know they want their product or service. They prey on that and blanket-market to them. As soon as you click on a link, BOOM, shitloads of spam emails come to you until you unsubscribe.

Marketers at one point knew people needed three touch points before they'd buy. Then it became seven, then 14 and now, it's become much more than that! Most people are now disengaged because they know clicking on a link will lead to constant spamming. It is called lead funnelling. They may have clicked on something initially because it looked interesting, even though they were not serious buyers. Then the robotic algorithms of the platforms keep sending more and more stuff their way. Again, they're hoping people click on the advert so they get paid, and to entice more impulse buying. The reason companies have done well over the years is that they know people buy with emotion and then justify with logic.

Companies bank on the rule of mass numbers and mass contacts to get the next sign-up. They don't care if you as an individual buy or not. It's a numbers game. Let's go fishing and see who takes the bait.

Nobody enjoys the feeling of missing out. 'Hurry, don't miss out!' 'Sale ends in 48 hours!' 'Limited stock'. Bla bla bla … Psychology selling plays with people's emotions. The tactic is to get you so emotionally involved that you want it, but instead of asking you to buy, the offer is taken away from you. You are made to feel that you can't have it, and then you want it even more and fight for the purchase. Obviously, the salesperson always allows you to buy or makes you feel special, letting you know that they can get one for you. But are you buying of your own free will? Well, you're made to think so!

After you've made the purchase, you feel good because you made the decision, but in fact, you've been emotionally manipulated into thinking you wanted it.

If you ever feel as if somebody is taking the prize away from you, proceed with caution. It's a really bad technique which many direct sales companies use to close a deal on the spot.

As mentioned earlier about 'telling is not selling', in leadership selling, information gathering is different from telling people what they want to hear. We, the salespeople, are just the facilitators. I know that as soon as I am being asked questions by the prospect, my job is to find out what the customer really wants to know. Are they buying or qualifying questions? You must be 100% knowledgeable about your product and service and clear on the outcome you want from the customer.

Just like Mr Maths Salesman was.

We purchased not because of his sales statistics or strategy, but because he demonstrated he understood our needs and what we wanted for our children, and he knew how his product would satisfy us. He had an answer for every question we asked. Indirectly, every question is an objection until agreed upon. My wife and I were satisfied with his answers to our problems and so we purchased.

I've seen this go the other way many times too.

A salesperson is asked questions and misinterprets what the customer is asking. The salesperson becomes frustrated and goes into defence mode, looking for angles that are irrelevant and becoming irritable and unfocused. They highlight other features that the customer is not interested in, simply because they do not understand the real objection/question.

I am repeating myself a lot in this book because repeating is how we learn. Sales is just a natural form of communication, except at the end, there is an exchange for money. To be a great salesperson, you must be a great communicator, a great leader and most importantly, a perfect listener!

When I am in the middle of a transaction, I'm listening for information from the customer. I understand that every objection is part of the communication and I work with the customer to discover their underlying needs. If I know I can help them solve a problem, then I know what I have is of value and service to them.

An objection is often not a true objection. It is typically a first sign of resistance as the customer works through the confusion in their mind until they fully understand.

The emotion is where the sale is made. That is why Mr Maths Salesperson kept asking us how we felt about something. It is the best question to ask — unlike the phone accessory salesperson who only cared about himself. As mentioned in a previous chapter, it is how you make a customer feel in a transaction that ensures its success.

A sales leader knows how to do this well.

When you come from a place of integrity with your selling, you will encounter fewer objections and more genuine conversations. It's the perfect scenario with sales.

THE GAME PART 3
ASKING FOR THE SALE — THE CLOSE

> 'You miss 100% of the shots you don't take.'
>
> **WAYNE GRETZKY**

Wrapping up a sale — or closing the deal as it's best known — should be as simple as 1, 2, 3. Yet it is where most salespeople make the biggest mistakes.

I learned early in my sales career to ask for the sale — because if you don't ask, you don't get. Seems pretty simple, right? Yet so many salespeople don't do it, which really surprises me. I've only ever had a handful of people ask me, 'Where do I sign?' and they're usually compulsive buyers. Most people wait to be led to the next step.

When you do not ask for the sale, you are doing your prospective buyer an injustice. If they don't purchase what you have, they could be missing out on so much more. Not asking for the sale also possibly highlights your lack of belief in what you are doing and the value you are adding.

I spoke about the fear aspect earlier, and to expand on that, you cannot miss what you have not done. That is why I love the quote above from Wayne Gretzky. Many salespeople freeze at the critical point, and subsequently don't get the deal.

The reason for this is their fear of losing the sale! They place attachment on the outcome of getting the sale, because they have lost sight of the service they are providing and are only thinking of themselves, the commission and what the deal is worth to them if they get it.

Many salespeople, in their minds, have already spent the commission before they get the sale. That is when things become awkward. If you follow through with the client's best intentions in mind, rather than yours, the final stage is easy. It is also important to make this step as simple as possible. For example, the maths tutor at the end of his presentation asked us if we were ready to get started. It's the perfect entrance to the final step. You could ask questions like, 'Would you like to give it a go?' Or, 'How many would you like?' Or, 'What plan fits you best?'

It is valuable to remember that 'you can't say the wrong thing to the right person'. You will know very quickly if you have a genuine buyer in front of you.

Interestingly, many salespeople regard the close as the final part of the sales process, where in fact, it is often only the beginning. Once the client is on board, there is generally a back-up service that comes from the company to follow through on what has been promised. In most cases, that service is carried out by other people in other departments, which could be an ongoing process. It all depends on if the sale was product or service based. That is why I label sales as a process. A close, to me, is like closing the door. It's done and dusted. That may very well be the case for the front-end salesperson whose sole purpose is to get the sale, but it is not so from the perspective of a business owner or a company.

Here is a cool little example.

Imagine yourself owning a restaurant. You start the sales process as soon as the patrons walk into your establishment. From there, the negotiation begins on where you will seat them. Once this is agreed, you ask them if they would like a drink or wish to see the menu. There will be objections while they make their decision. They will ask you buying questions, you will listen to their interests and provide feedback on the menu.

Now the service begins.

The back-up or follow-on service is all part of the sale, as you now need to deliver on the goods. The waiter asks them what they feel like eating and if they would like anything to go with the food. Are they after just drinks, or entree and dessert too? It is a basic conversation.

That's as simple as it needs to be in any sale.

Never underestimate the importance of asking for the sale. It is a crucial part of the process to ask for permission to continue. You know that you are genuinely coming from a place of service, and so it is practically your obligation to do so.

What excites me the most is when they ask you what is next. You then explain the steps that happen after they get started, and continue to answer their questions. You know you have shown great leadership and done a great job when this happens. Yet, as mentioned earlier, that does not happen often and if you rely on it to get your sales, then you will ultimately starve. Never just expect or assume. I have been caught out before and it's extremely uncomfortable. Nine out of ten times, there is no return. It is common courtesy to *ask* for the business, so make it a must in your process.

As explained about trial closing in previous chapters and getting a 'yes' when communicating with people, each time you get a yes, you close another door. Once all the doors are closed and it's time to go to the next step, you should only take them there if you genuinely believe they are ready and that you can deliver on what has been spoken about. Ask yourself: when you are ready to buy, do you like being asked? Then, once you agree, are you more open to formalising the negotiations?

The contractual obligations or paperwork is another place where deals can be lost if salespeople do not close doors properly along the way. If a prospective client freaks out when you're doing the paperwork, you've made a very big mistake in having them there in the first place.

You need to be able to confidently guide the purchasers through the paperwork. It is all a process — from where they are now to where they want to be, and how your product or service will get them there. If you are afraid of what is in the paperwork, so should your customer be! Some fine print can be dodgy. If you are with an organisation that has this, get out. You must show integrity from start to finish and well beyond. I've seen salespeople afraid of losing a deal because of the paperwork and if that could lose you a deal, you should not get to that stage to begin with.

If all is well with the paperwork, then that part of the process is a breeze. All you need to do is simplify it and ensure you explain it all clearly. Make it light, explain any official terms and clarify any standard wording as being common to all similar transactions. Again, your job is to make the consumer feel comfortable, and to have no attachment to the outcome.

When a sale is done the right way, at the end of the transaction a buyer should feel excited. They are purchasing something they want. The seller should also feel excited, not because they got a sale, but because they orchestrated a deal that has made somebody else happy and they have been of genuine service. Imagine that — feeling good because you've made somebody else feel good! What a world you now live in.

> This reminds me of my introduction to direct sales when I sold property seminar programs. We would do a one-hour-plus consultation and expect to close the sale at the end. We did the presentation in such a way that it was extremely uncomfortable for the customer to leave until they signed on the dotted line. I was always labelled 'the closer'. After the consult, when others asked how I'd gone, my answer was always, 'Yep, got them!'

Makes me sick now thinking of it, but it was what it was back then, and it has led me down the path to a whole new way of delivering to people. Take it from me: being a closer is not what it's about and it never should be. Dangling the carrot then taking it away from people, using tricks of mind manipulation, bullying people to buy ... it's all just crap. Working with the customer, understanding their needs and being the facilitator, sometimes even the matchmaker for their problems, that's true leadership and authentic selling.

Sales can be a lucrative and rewarding career. Many people make a lot of money being in sales and there is nothing wrong with that. I must admit, I chose sales for that reason. The difference maker is when you lead with your heart and not your head. It took me a long time to really mature and work out the lay of the land and my spiritual journey here on planet earth. I spent many years working out my purpose and while I learned this at my second Anthony Robbins seminar, it was not until 15-odd years later that I understood it.

> 'The purpose of my life is to be successful and fulfilled. To enjoy being happy, healthy and loving and to appreciate myself and others.'
>
> **ADAM BUDE**

There is a lot to be grateful for. The way many sales are conducted worldwide is simply rubbish. I would truly like to see a higher level of sales, where the hard sell is gone and authentic selling, genuine selling and leadership selling take over.

The feeling of wanting to buy is beautiful. The feeling of wanting to serve is even better. Get out of your own way, leave your ego at the door and believe in yourself and your abilities to make a difference.

Together, we can change the way things are done, one person at a time.

Please pay it forward and give a copy of this book to anybody you know who is in sales or who owns a business. I know that if everybody who reads this from cover to cover takes just one simple thing from it, collectively we will create a better world to work in. People will again be empowered to make their own choices, and organisations will thrive because their intentions are about being of service.

So, are you ready to roll up your sleeves and lead authentically with your customers' best interests in mind, being the salesperson that you would love to buy from?

MY RECOMMENDED READING LIST

Ask and It Is Given by Esther & Jerry Hicks
Awaken the Giant Within by Anthony Robbins
Breaking the Habit of Being Yourself by Dr Joe Dispenza
Born to Run by Christopher McDougall
Can't Hurt Me by David Goggins
Chicken Soup for the Soul by Jack Canfield
Dare to Lead by Brene Brown
Don't Sweat the Small Stuff by Richard Carlson
Eat That Frog by Brian Tracy
Find Your Why by Simon Sinek
Finding Flow: The Psychology of Engagement With Everyday Life by Mihaly Csikszentmihalyi
Go for No!: Yes Is the Destination, No Is How You Get There by Andrea Waltz and Richard Fenton
Go-Giver by Bob Burg and John David Mann
How the Best Leaders Lead by Brian Tracy
How to Master the Art of Selling by Tom Hopkins
How to Win Friends and Influence People by Dale Carnegie
It's Not About the Money by Bob Proctor
Living the 7 Habits by Stephen R. Covey
Master Your Time, Master Your Life by Brian Tracy

Me, Inc. by Gene Simmons
No Excuses! : The Power of Self-Discipline by Brian Tracy
Power vs Force by Dr. David R. Hawkins
Purple Cow by Seth Godin
Rich Dad, Poor Dad by Robert Kiyosaki
Sales Dogs by Blair Singer
Secrets of Closing the Sale by Zig Ziglar
SPIN Selling by Neil Rackham
Success Through a Positive Mental Attitude
    by W Clement Stone and Napoleon Hill
Synchrodestiny by Deepak Chopra
The 21 Irrefutable Laws of Leadership by John C. Maxwell
The 7 Habits of Highly Effective People by Stephen Covey
The Alchemist by Paulo Coelho
The Greatest Salesman In the World by Og Mandino
The Magic of Thinking Big by David Schwartz
The Magician's Way by William Whitecloud
The Four-Hour Work Week by Tim Ferriss
The NLP Coach by Ian McDermott & Wendy Jago
The One Minute Manager by Ken Blanchard
The One-Minute Millionaire by Mark Victor Hansen
The Power of Ambition by Jim Rohn
The Power of Intention by Wayne Dyer
The Power of Now by Eckhart Tolle
The Power of Vulnerability by Brene Brown
The Psychology of Selling by Brian Tracy
The Psychology of Selling by Brian Tracy
The Richest Man in Babylon by George S. Clason
The Science of Getting Rich by Wallace D. Wattles
The Science of Selling by David Hoffeld

MY RECOMMENDED READING LIST

The Secret by Rhonda Byrne
*The Subtle Art of Not Giving a F*ck* by Mark Manson
The Universe Has Your Back by Gabrielle Bernstein
The Way of the Peaceful Warrior by Dan Millman
Think and Grow Rich by Napoleon Hill
To Sell Is Human by Daniel H. Pink
Turning Passions into Profits by Christopher Howard
Way of The Peaceful Warrior by Dan Millman
Who Moved My Cheese by Spencer Johnson
Your Network Is Your Net Worth by Porter Gale

www.ingramcontent.com/pod-product-compliance
Lightning Source LLC
Chambersburg PA
CBHW021408290426
44108CB00010B/436